PARIS ALBUM

Jean Cocteau was a French poet and writer whose originality, versatility and vast output in almost every art form have made his name known throughout the world. The friend, and often collaborator, of writers, musicians, painters, choreographers and film directors, he appears to have found the secret of eternal youth in switching from one 'manner' to another.

He was particularly interested in the cinema, and his *Le Sang d'un poète* is a classic example of a French avant-garde film. Of the many films which he wrote or directed, the most remarkable are *L'Eternel Retour, La Belle et La Bête, Orphée* and *Le Testament d'Orphée*.

His best known books include *La Machine Infernale* and *Les Enfants Terribles. Paris Album, 1900–1914* which he wrote in 1956, originally appeared as short articles in *Le Figaro*. He died of a heart attack on 11 October, 1963.

PARIS ALBUM

1900–1914

JEAN COCTEAU

With the author's original illustrations

Translated from the French by
Margaret Crosland

A COMET BOOK

A Comet Book
Published in 1987
by the Paperback Division of
W.H. Allen & Co. Plc
44 Hill Street, London W1X 8LB

First published in France by Editions Bernard Grasset
under the title *Portraits-Souvenir*
First published in Great Britain by
W.H. Allen & Co Plc in 1956

Printed in Great Britain by
Mackays of Chatham Ltd, Kent

ISBN 0 86379 139 5

CONTENTS

TO
MARCEL KHILL

JE SUIS UN MENSONGE QUI DIT
TOUJOURS LA VÉRITÉ—
   from *Opéra* by Jean Cocteau.

TRANSLATOR'S NOTE

MANY of Cocteau's books are autobiographical in character, but none so directly and lightheartedly as *Portraits-Souvenir*, this album of memories originally described and drawn for the Paris newspaper *Le Figaro*. All Cocteau's family are here, and that other family of "sacred monsters" whom Cocteau brought into his personal mythology and took through life with him—including the great actresses, Réjane, Sarah Bernhardt; the lesser known but eccentric and vivid Edouard de Max; the galaxy of stage stars including Mistinguett, Polaire, Sacha Guitry; writers of such varying calibre as Jules Lemaître, Catulle Mendès, Anna de Noailles, Colette as a young girl, Edmond Rostand; the brilliant caricaturist Sem; musicians such as Sarasate or Reynaldo Hahn; the mysterious Dargelos, schoolboy hero of Cocteau's most famous novel *Les Enfants Terribles*. Cocteau recaptures, too, all the thrills of the circus and the stage adaptation of *Round the World in Eighty Days* which awakened his passion for "the great golden forbidden theatres".

Cocteau is aware of the slightest manifestation of fashion and believes in its poetic reality; in this book he describes how the world of 1900, with its *cocottes* and *demi-castors* waltzing at the skating-rink, became twenty years later, the world of Paul Poiret clothes, the tango and the fox-trot. He mentions obscure plays by obscure authors, recalls events which made news, such as the disastrous fire at the Bazaar de la Charité, and lets unexpected floodlights play over a vanished world.

It is *La Difficulté d'Etre,* that autobiography of a different kind, that Cocteau regards as the key to his house. *Paris Album* is the façade, and there are many windows looking into the rooms, some dark, some brilliantly lit. Many of Cocteau's favourite themes, the function of the poet, the value of acrobatics, the power of the "sacred monsters", are evoked not in the abstract but as part of his own experience. Cocteau has often been criticized as out of touch with reality, and even his "exact" poets walk "some distance above the ground on quickly-melting snow". In *Paris Album* Cocteau's feet are sometimes on the ground, sometimes on the tightrope; like Anna de Noailles he juggles with words, lifts cardboard weights and sometimes falls. But like his acrobats he despises the no-man's-land of the safety-net.

Many friends have helped me with the twice-ravelled knots of this translation. I should like especially to thank Mr Sinclair Road for his many constructive suggestions.

M. C.

INTRODUCTION

IT seems to me impossible to write memoirs. In the first place, I mix up dates, perhaps jumping ten years and placing people in settings that belong to others. Memory is a terrible, obscure night into which I ought not to venture for fear of incurring the penalty of the archæologists who violate Egyptian burial chambers—for tombs take their revenge. There exists a kind of sleep which rejects the sacrilege of light and exudes evil. No, it would certainly be more reasonable and less funereal to play Aunt Sally the wrong way round, making my figures stand up rather than knocking them down, aiming the balls in such a way that faces loom up out of the darkness with the places and circumstances fastened round them, like the Managers in *Parade* whom Picasso dressed in a perspective of Paris and New York.

I have in mind the sort of costume found in the booths of fairground photographers. The customer puts his head through a huge painted collar and is uprooted, transported behind an aeroplane propeller or flung into a Serpollet car or a boxing ring. The souvenir portraits I would like to take are different— the customer must create his own reality and prevent me from confusing dates and backgrounds, a confusion which is the essence of those amusing fairground pictures but which hardly contributes to my search for exactness.

A poet is the vehicle and natural medium for unknown forces that possess him and take advantage of his purity to spread themselves throughout the world; they cannot solve the problems against which we are all on guard from the moment we awake; but at least they can put them before us until we are sick of them.

Barely do we open our eyes in the morning, after the atrocious amalgam of dreams, than we try to forget that order of things in which the poet is a specialist, things that make him the ideal type of "undesirable". Among all the charges levelled against him, is not one of the most serious the charge of exactness? The poet is exact. Poetry is exactness. Since the time of Baudelaire the public has gradually come to realize that poetry is one of the most insolent ways of telling the truth. No weapon is more precise, and it is through an instinctive movement of self-defence, caused by their terror of exactness and revealing light, that the mass of people continue to confuse poetry with lies and quickness of mind with paradox.

What is the point of telling a story that does not carry within itself the inimitable weight of truth? What is the point of imaginary memoirs, untrue anecdotes, sentences put in wrong mouths, or picture-esque recollections? The dead weight of inexactness overwhelms everyone with fatigue. Very different is the searchlight beam that plays across the darkness accumulated behind each one of us and picks out a significant countenance, deed or place, imbuing it with all possible expressive strength and resurrected life.

INTRODUCTION

I want to collect my souvenir portraits by losing the thread. I mean by this that the thread of chronological order would vanish in the distorting mirror of memory, but it would only appear to be lost. In this way perhaps I could employ a more lively and less pretentious method of searching the void.

Poets possess only intimate memories. No secretary can reply to the strange messages and cries addressed to them from distant rooms by those unknown friends recruited through books who are after all the only excuse for writing. Let me add that poets walk some distance above the ground on quickly-melting snow, into which their footprints disappear. All this does not make the work of remembering and resuscitating ghosts any easier. At this dangerous pastime, as we turn towards the past which lies in flames, we run the risk of being turned into a pillar of salt—a pillar of tears.

1934-5. A curtain falls, a curtain rises. Life is dead, long live life. One age is dead, an age when I lived dangerously, against my will and with all my strength; now my antennæ tell me a new age is beginning, and I catch a glimpse of nobility, and the signs please me. I take advantage of a moment's *entr'acte* to stand up, relax, turn round and look about through my opera glasses.

I have known many singular faces and places which I set opposite the plural mass; they dwell within me but play no active part in the preoccupations which guide me and line my road. Looking back at those "stars" in the Paris sky, those sacred monsters—

places or persons—I realize above all that the originality of their appearance (which distinguished them
from others, threw them into relief and made them
into personalities), arose not so much from a desire
to stand out, but from a struggle with death; a
pathetic struggle that enlarged them and made them
as different from mere caricatures as a gentleman
walking with tiny steps and carrying a Japanese
parasol in his hand differs from an acrobat walking
with the same steps and brandishing the same parasol
on a tight-rope.

In other words I have only retained memories of
individuals and groups who were desperate for sur-
vival, whose frivolity arose from tragedy, whose
lightness was prodigious and whose silhouettes, to
use the expression of Thomas Mann in that masterpiece
The Magic Mountain, were silhouettes on a grand scale.

Souvenir portraits on a grand scale. That is a project
that tempts me. I wonder if I can pull it off? I know I
must plan nothing in advance, or predetermine what
to say, but that I must lean out into the darkness first.

For I disapprove of the mixture of forms; a play
should be a play, a film a film, a novel a novel and an
article an article.

One day when I was reading to Picasso a letter full
of insults he said to me: "That's an anonymous
letter", and when I showed him that it was signed, he
added: "It doesn't matter. The anonymous letter is a
form." That is why I composed a spoken song, *Anna
la Bonne*. The song is a form. Whether it is sung or
recited, it is neither a monologue nor a poem; it

remains a song. An article is a form. It should be like nothing else.

A week-end article for a newspaper, an article by a reminiscent poet—I see this as something light and racy, written with fresh ink on the edge of an editorial desk in a newspaper office, without any retouching, without any link with literary politics, on the surface of the period and all periods, participating in the laughter which has been the privilege of all serious minds and which reveals us our subject to his very soul.

Just as only bogus gravity knows nothing of laughter, bogus great epochs despise the lightness, the intoxicating froth and the supreme elegance of other epochs which are lofty and tragic.

Shall I admit that this new epoch, this new age which I foresee gives me great hope and much excitement? If I were young and rich I would cross the Place Vendôme tomorrow in a dashing fiacre, take the Place de la Concorde and the Champs-Elysées and reach the *Figaro* office where the young dandy George Sand climbed the steps with her cigar in her mouth, and I would try to look like Amy Boisseau's charming colossus, the Barber of Seville who guards the door with a bronze guitar slung over his shoulder. Covered with bronze hairnets and bronze pompoms, he trims the bronze barbs of his bronze pen and sharpens it carefully with a bronze razor blade.

I

CHILDHOOD

THE Paramount is the ghost of the Vaudeville. On the scene of the crime, where this queen among music-halls was murdered by commerce, at the corner of the boulevard where beat this red and gold heart, gilded and adored by the Paris of my childhood, near the pavement where Réjane's mules used to wait with her cab, day and night the Paramount looms up, lunar and terrible, with its huge ghosts who talk and its orchestra that rises from the depths. The Parisian passes quickly and crosses himself. He misses the excellent Vaudeville auditorium, one of the three or four which possessed through some unknown happy chance the excellence that cannot be obtained to order and should be protected like the trees in the squares, the lungs of a capital city. Apart from the three official theatres there remain only the Variétés, the Ambigu, the Gymnase and the Bouffes-Parisiens.

I used to advise young people who wanted to understand the prestige of the old Vaudeville before it was destroyed to go and hear Madame Pitoëff before her husband ended the exhausting sacrifice to which she was condemned by her role in *Ce Soir on Improvise*. She told the story of the theatre to her children dressed in their nightgowns. I do not think there can ever have been a more intense plea in favour of those old theatres which are so desperately in danger from the modern love for the necropolis of the cinema.

Like a charming little skull set lightly on some scarecrow in a long black smock—it would scare anything in the world except the birds—Madame Pitoëff imitated the great heroines of the boards. She conjured up the chandeliers, the elegant darkness and the canvas painted with long draperies which rose over the sunshine of the drama.

The curtain at the Comédie-Française for the classical matinées, the wait for the three fateful knocks before *Œdipe Roi*, the glow of the curtain at the Châtelet, her mica monocle, the figures-of-eight made by the man spraying the proscenium with water, the caramel-seller in the interval, the orchestra playing the prelude—a host of memories shot through me as I saw the actress lose all reserve until she was consumed in the very fire of professional hell.

Another theatre in danger was the small hall in the Conservatoire de Musique. My grandfather owned seats there in the third row of the orchestra stalls, on the right. In that painted wooden sarcophagus filled with venerable mummies, I discovered Beethoven, Liszt, Berlioz and Wagner all in a jumble. That hall was a miracle of another sort. If children missed the theatre curtain, the fragile scarlet wall and the sudden footlights, the flaming sword of the archangel at the gates of Paradise, they could look with surprise at the tiered seats and the unashamed bustle of the choir, who, with beards and gold-rimmed spectacles, princess tunics with yellow bows on the shoulders, and black

mon
souvenir
de
Réjane

Jean

velvet ribbons round their necks, took their seats and gossiped, before the organ note which was cruelly prolonged by the conductor until the last person coughed and the poor short-sighted lady, overcome with shame, at last found the number of her seat and eventually sat down.

My mother, when she was a little girl, watched the Vaudeville being built over the débris of the rue Basse-du-Rempart. Beloved Vaudeville, that I saw demolished and assassinated, just like the Pavillon de Hanovre opposite, where the ghost with its grottoes, labyrinths, aquariums, Mickey Mouse shows and bird cages, mercury lights and water games is just as alarming as the ghost of the Paramount. My grand-parents lived opposite, in the rue de la Chaussée d'Antin, on the fourth floor, next door to Winter-halter. On the first floor in the same building lived the Rossinis. The Rossinis received many grand gentle-men and fine ladies, and Madame Rossini, who was afraid of tobacco, like Madame Fenouillard among the Sioux, sent the gentlemen to smoke up on the fourth floor. My grandmother put up with the smell of smoke for the sake of music. Madame Rossini was a thin, unpleasant woman. When she was offered *foie gras* at dinner with Gustave de Rothschild, she refused it, saying: "No, thank you! I do not eat animals' diseases", while she crushed bread on the tablecloth with her lorgnette for her toothless little dog. Rossini terrified my mother. In the mornings my grandfather made her carry a basket of eggs up to him, and pushed her into his bedroom. On the piano she caught sight of a series of wigs destined for the monumental egg that emerged from the blankets and eiderdowns. These wigs, arranged on stands, varied from short to long hair. The maestro wore them one after the other, until the hairdresser paid his imaginary visit.

One of these wigs, in its oval green box, became one of the fetiches of my childhood, the object of furtive hunts in my grandfather's dressing room, when the sound of the string quartet assured me that he would not come to surprise me and I could rummage round at leisure. For these quartets, like a halo round the Rossinis, created a musical atmosphere throughout the building I never knew. It spread to 45 rue La Bruyère where throughout my childhood we lived in a large two-storied house. The courtyard looked on to the Gaveau gardens (music again!). My grandparents lived on the floor above, in an apartment which the capricious architect had laid out in such a way that we had to walk down corridors and climb up and down steep staircases in order to go from one room to another. This apartment was ideal for the scampering games and fantasies of childhood. I have inserted this background into my dreams so often and added so many complications to it that I can no longer see it in its true perspective. It has left the apartment, taken off from the ground and floated away like a Montgolfier balloon. I can remember our apartment and our bed-rooms and far, far away, in another world, in some unreal and fabulous region, the apartment where my grandfather possessed a silver bath resonant as a gong and filled with shoes and books. He collected Greek busts, drawings by Ingres, pictures by Delacroix, Florentine coins, ministers' autographs, masks from Antinous, vases from Cyprus and Stradivarius violins.

I liked best the glass cases with the masks and the violins. Behind the glass, the Antinous masks, with their enamel eyes, pale terra cotta cheeks and horse-shoe beards, sat on the red velvet like people in a theatre box painted by Manet. The violins adorned the billiard room. They were embedded in royal blue velvet on the ebony furniture, the drawers of which contained rosin, cords, violin strings and billiard chalks. For these treasures were used. Even the sacred Stradivariuses, which became resonant when another Stradivarius was played anywhere else (*sic*), left their blue velvet on the evenings when the string quartet assembled: Sarasate, Sivori, Grébert and their music-loving host Eugène Lecomte. On these evenings of chamber music the great game for my cousins and myself was to crawl the entire length of the ceremonial staircase which linked the two floors together. The magic, which, I repeat, situated the apartment outside space, made this staircase a place unto itself, entirely self-sufficient, its supreme limit being a gate which my grandfather had fitted to stop us from falling down.

The game consisted then in waiting for Sarasate to arrive, hiding behind a halberd standard lamp in red plush which was used in the "poor prisoner" game, and while later he tidied his hair in front of the mirror in the ante-room, seizing the opportunity of closing the gate and thus obtaining the picture *Animal Tamer in his Cage*.

When he was behind the bars we thought that Sarasate, with his big moustaches, his grey mane of hair, his braided frock coat, his watch chains, his trousers with their understraps and his little patent leather boots looked like a lion dressed up as a lion tamer, and this satisfied our craving for cartoon films and exaggerated caricatures before they existed.

In fact the real show, the real picture game, took place during the holidays at Maisons-Laffitte. The Château of Maisons-Laffitte adorns a huge park of lime trees, lawns, flower beds, fountains, white gates, tennis courts, racehorses, cyclists and middle-class houses. With Aimé Simon-Girard I used to cycle hard to the forest of Saint Germain to smoke in secret some revolting snuff in horsechestnuts hollowed out in the shape of a pipe with a stem made from an elder twig. Afterwards we would go down on all fours and chew the grass to avoid smelling of tobacco.

The trainers lived a gay life. Max Lebaudy, who was called *le petit sucrier*, had his carriages washed in champagne and organised corridas. We saw Madame du Gast, president of the Society for the Protection of Animals, being arrested by the police. There were gymkhanas with sack races and ladies with beribboned rabbits on leads.

On Sundays, early in the morning, my grandfather, in his tussore jacket, with his straw hat on the back of his head, and carrying a little bunch of primroses in his hand, would wait in the Place Sully, which was adorned in the centre with a gas-lamp and a bed of begonias, and watch the roads which came up from

le Corset "droit
a maisons laffitte

... ladies with beribboned rabbits on leads

the racecourse. All at once, in the pitiless sunshine, the virtuosi would arrive. They came in an open fiacre, with no coachman. The fiacre of Fantomas is driven by dead men. The fiacre of the virtuosi! Melpomene or some allegorical musical figure must have reigned invisible on the seat.

Sarasate, his right foot on his left knee, his shoulders resting against the back cushions, wearing an opera hat, a frock coat and leather gloves, held the reins and guided the equipage from the back seat. As soon as they arrived the fiacre was unharnessed, the horse, desperate with fatigue, was fed on a soup of warm burgundy and carrots, and the virtuosi lunched. Sivori was a dwarf. At table my grandmother made

le fiacre des virtuoses

Saluts à Jean ✶
ma grand mère

. . . still playing, leaning forward into space

him sit on musical scores. "Not on Beethoven, madame", he could cry. "Not on Beethoven", and he speared strawberries with his toothpick. My grandfather cut up his meat with that same gesture he would later use to attack a bar of music with his sporting bow. This chamber music was in no way music to be listened to or music to please, but music to be played and beaten out, with nods of the head. A sport, a form of exercise like any other: fencing, rowing, boxing. There was something for everyone. It brought old friends together, prevented quarrels between them, guaranteed that we could hunt through forbidden rooms without fear of disturbance, and supplied us with fits of giggling and charades.

le violon de le roreine!

... tore his hair and cried in his guttural voice

Grébert played the 'cello. Whenever my grandmother passed on tip-toe through the far end of the room, with her knitting in her hand, he would stand up and bow to her, still playing, leaning forward into space.

After the quartet, our virtuosi would disguise themselves in whatever came to hand and go to the house of the lady doctor Gache-Sarrothe, the inventor of the straight corset and a neighbour in the Place Sully, to serenade her. Twilight fell. The Great Bear shone over the garden. The heliotropes were watered and revived. We had dinner, and we children were put in a dining-room called the "punishment room", where my cousin Pierre refused to eat from any plates except those marked with the initial of Napoléon. After dinner the gentlemen seasoned meerschaum pipes, and Sarasate recounted his conquests of Europe. He used to show us a little gold coffin on the end of a chain that contained a tiny realistic violin given to him by the Queen of Spain. One evening the realistic tiny violin fell into a glass of beer, and we tried to fish it out with a straw. Amid the general consternation Sarasate tore his hair and cried in his guttural voice: "The queen's violin! The queen's violin."

Those were moments which served no other purpose except that of illuminating the angle from which children watch grown-ups, by means of bribes, on all fours, behind kitchen doors and on the stairs, with eyes that accept nothing except poetic intensity.

II

THE THEATRE

THE Theatre! Evenings at the Comédie-Française and evenings at the Opéra!

This is what used to happen. I watched my mother dress. A cloud of perfume and mauve powder scented the room and the semi-darkness between the chintzes with their multi-coloured designs of exotic trees and birds of paradise. Beyond the open door the brilliant gas-light in the dressing-room illuminated the wardrobe and the mirror which reflected the scene in greater beauty and depth. It was in this mirror that I watched the preparations. My mother, who looked slim, monumental and shorter than normal from where I sat between the chest of drawers and the fireplace, seemed to be held up by her long stiff Raudnitz gown in red velvet embroidered with jet, with leg of mutton sleeves; her arms, shoulders and neck glimmered palely above the red velvet draped over her plain corsage, and at any moment, I thought, this velvet might turn into the back of the Comédie-Française stage seen against the edge of the boxes: a tortoiseshell fan, the quiver of black lace, the mother of pearl lorgnette is raised, discreet applause. This at least is what I imagined, during the ceremonial fitting of the long gloves which were so difficult to put on; they were like dead skins which began to live, cling and

ma mère s'habille pour aller voir l'Énigme

... conferred on my mother the nobility of a Spanish Virgin

take shape, as each finger was fitted in turn; and then finally came that adorable rite, that feminine gesture immortalised by Mayol, of buttoning the little skylight at the wrist, and I would kiss the exposed palm. It was the end of the show, the prologue to the real show for which all this elegance was invented, and the wardrobe mirror revealed my mother to me—what am I saying, revealed a madonna encased in velvet, strangled with diamonds, emplumed with a nocturnal aigrette, a glittering chestnut bristling with rays of light, tall, distrait, torn between her last reminders that I should be good and her last glance in the mirror. Kneeling prostrate on the floor the maid spread out the train of the dress and finally conferred on my mother the nobility of a Spanish Virgin. Next a fur coat concealed the clusters and darts of light, mother bent down, kissed me rapidly and left for that murmuring ocean of jewels, feathers and heads, where she was to pour herself out like a red river and mingle her velvet with the velvet of the theatre, her glitter with the glitter of the chandelier and the girandole.

I dreamt of the theatre. With the help of these departures and prefigurative comparisons I imagined it inaccurately. When my brother Paul was taken—to *Samson and Delilah*, if I remember rightly—I consoled myself a little by the fact that one of us was embarking on the red river and that perhaps I would embark in my turn and come to know the great golden forbidden theatre.

My mother and father went to the Comédie-Française or to the Opéra. On the opera evenings they

took with them the scores of *The Mastersingers* or *Tannhaüser*. The Comédie-Française gave *La Grève des Forgerons*. Mounet-Sully declaimed, alone, before a tribunal of subscribers who were present in scarlet, ermine and judges' caps, the interminable poem which begins "Your honours, my story is brief"; and the memory of this wonderful monologue-play was not without its influence on me when I decided to read

scène d'amour
aux "Français"

. . . hid her trouble from Raphael Duflos

La Voix Humaine to the reading committee of the Comédie-Française.

On the programme with *La Grève* was *L'Enigme* by

Paul Hervieu. I knew *L'Enigme* through an exquisite caricature by Cappiello, published in the magazine *Le Théâtre*. The hooknosed profile of the divine Madame Bartet, who looked like a young owl, and the horse-faced profile of Marthe Brandès faced each other on a staircase in a castle. *Whose lover was he?* In one hand both ladies held a little lamp with a globe, and with the other they clutched at negligés trimmed with frills and *broderie anglaise*.

This was the era of problem plays, when Bertha Cerny hid her trouble from Raphael Duflos by picking up her skirts, stretching her leg out and exposing the sole of her right foot to the blazing logs in a monumental fireplace. The grown-ups avoided discussing the problem of the play in our presence: it was with the assistance of Cappiello's astonishing synthesis—apart from achieving a perfect likeness his Japanese pencil endowed actresses with the beauty of flora or fauna, tigers or orchids—through cryptic remarks heard at table and through postcards that my brother hid in his school books, that I combined these plays into one solitary spectacle, which owed something to Guignol, the staircase in the rue La Bruyère and Mass at the church of La Trinité. This spectacle contributed the intrigues, characters and fantastic décors to the theatres we built out of cardboard boxes from Old England, and made me welcome the exciting fever of measles, scarlet fever or appendicitis. (Old England, where they sold sailor suits with whistles, putty-coloured monkey-jackets and revolting gaiters which were lined with red flannel and scratched our legs, occupied an important place in our childish lives.)

Convalescence ended in the sunshine in the courtyard of No. 45. We hammered, stuck things together, cut things up, painted them, invented footlights made out of candles and prompter's boxes which opened and closed. My German nursemaid Josephine sewed the costumes. This craze for building theatres in the courtyard, decorating them and lighting them, lasted until the Lycée Condorcet period, when thanks to certain gifts from heaven and because of Fraülein Josephine, I carried off the dunce's prizes for German, drawing and gymnastics, disgracing by my absurd presence the platform of honour and the Saint-Charlemagne banquet.

René Rocher, my classmate, supported my enterprises. Now that he directs real theatres, he will remember our courtyard at 45 rue La Bruyère. There was a heap of untidiness in the middle. At the right-hand side we found nails and planks in a shed; it was an old stable. Above each empty box you could read the horses' names: Gamin, Mascotte. On the left, behind an ivy-coloured wall, we could hear the hose-pipe washing down the victoria of the Comte and Comtesse de Crèvecoeur.

Good heavens, how few entertainments there were in those days! As children we were intoxicated with unending spectacles, but the poor grown-ups who disliked staying at home and did not possess our mysterious resources had the choice between Yvette Guilbert, *La Marche à l'Etoile* at the Théâtre d'Ombres Chinoises, Robert Houdin, *Théodora* with Sarah

Bernhardt, *Le Nouveau Jeu* with Lavallière, *La Citoyenne Cotillon* with Granier, *Le Duel* with Le Bargy, and Guitry in *L'Assommoir* (or some programme of that sort). And it pleased, it lasted, and there were no films, no dance halls, no real music halls.

Those superb resounding blows administered by Françoise Rosay to her godson in Feyder's film *Pension Mimosas* should be applied to those pessimists who continually repeat: "There's nothing to see at the theatre or the cinema, nothing's going on, no one gives us anything. . . ." For where is that innocent age when we saw *L'Arroseur Arrosé, Le Bock* and *Bébés au Bord de l'Eau*, in the cellar of the Frères Lumière, near Old England?

Nowadays, the comfortable darkness is full of obedient talking ghosts, alabaster statues which speak and move, and dead heroines; Hokusai's *Wave* looks like a poor coloured unanimated cartoon. And without mentioning the theatres which abound in works where the genius of modern actors would suffice to make the boredom of the public ridiculous, I am amazed by the countless distractions embroidered into the train of our beautiful city, and I listen to that collection of affecting young women, blondes, brunettes and red-heads, who sing love songs, Damia, Fréhel, Lucienne Boyer, Lys Gauty, Oswald. Their songs, which are almost anonymous, must have been discovered ready-made by water diviners, famous in advance, waiting to gush out from the pavements of capital cities.

I thought of this wealth of shows, big and small, this prodigality offered by a city of genius in return for so much ingratitude, when one Sunday evening at the Salle Pleyel, Serge Lifar appeared between the vast curtains wearing the blood-red tunic of Apollo Musagetes, escorted by Russian ghosts, glistening with dramatic solitude, and bringing with him an atmosphere of *crime passionnel*.

Lifar, Al Brown and Greta Garbo and all the stars of the stage, the boxing ring and the cinema, and even the mannequins from a fashion show at Chanel's who look like jockeys and could be their own horses circling round a paddock of mirrors—I used to tell myself that they too came out of a fairytale, that in order to move they possess the secret power of thunder and its terrifying roguishness, that the public suspects them as much as poets, that the masses adore them, detest them and watch for the slightest lapse, and before they can give us any pleasure we must cultivate and rediscover the childhood that poets prolong until death and grown-ups in towns pride themselves on having lost.

III

ROUND THE WORLD IN EIGHTY DAYS

I HOPE to be read by people who remain children in spite of everything. I find one in a thousand. Eyes that can see into that first fairyland give better protection against the indignities of old age than any beauty treatment or diet. But alas, the people who wish to live as warmly protected in this credulous fairyland as in their mother's womb are hurt by our nerve-wracking age, with its fidgety untidiness, twitching lights, traffic and all its pretexts for dividing oneself in two and tearing oneself away from other people and from oneself.

Every child wants a room of his own in which to keep his toys and loves together. He detests whatever scatters them. He likes illnesses, which bring them together and protect them. I nurtured my phobia about going away, and about places where I could not imagine the people I loved, to the extent of worshipping thunderstorms. The gentle sound of April thunder, like a game of bowls, gentle Sunday thunder arranging the furniture in heaven—I still worship it. Thunder was the sign that plans for a boating expedition would be abandoned, the assurance that the family would stay at home, that my cousins would help me build up my bricks, that the nursemaids would sit in a circle and sew, that I would hear the quartet

and later the click of billiard balls downstairs, proving
that the grown-ups were still children.

I hated all circumstances which forced me on

Le billard

jean

Sunday to come out of my comfortable nest of
dreams, which *la séquestrée de Poitiers* was one day to
call her *"chère petite grotte"*, her *"cher grand-fond Malam-
pia"*—all except two: one which sprang from the
grown-ups' displeasure, and one from their pleasure.
These two exceptional circumstances led to a game of
"little death", an exquisite agony that was self-
induced, longed-for, concealed, feared and complex
in the extreme. Pride, the shame of being rewarded or
punished, had no place in it. These circumstances
prolonged the dreams of both country and town
Sundays. In one way they provided a rest for me, by

substituting an accidental and unpredictable fairyland for my intimate methods, the first of which was to hold a cup of revolting liquid in my right hand, a peppermint in my left, and refuse to take my Sunday morning purge. Everyone pleaded, I refused; they insisted, I refused; they begged, I refused. The moment my mother's angry expression contradicted the bribery of her charming voice and her hand struck my cheek, the "little death" began to work.

Although I knew the plot, the "little death" came and took me by surprise. She took me on her shoulders in a sack. Pierre Barrère, my grandfather's bewhiskered servant (he used to eat live snails and crunch up the shells), disguised himself as Mother Lachique. After a short dramatic scene he put me in the sack and ran up and down the stairs until I felt lost and everything seemed unrecognizable. I believed it all, I enjoyed my terror. My heart beat faster, my tongue went dry, my ears throbbed and I came out of the sack drunk with darkness, jolts and dreams, ready to refuse the purge, after really crossing the river of the dead, clutching my obol—a half-melted peppermint—in my hand.

In town the "little death" arose from a reward—seats at the theatre. We were going to the theatre! Hardly had I learnt the news when the mechanism came into operation. A dark unending corridor, a "little death" corridor, took shape in my feverish night, crossed Sunday morning and came out in full daylight, opposite the courtroom of the box-office and the black-coated judges of the matinée at the Châtelet or the New Circus.

La mère
Lachique
m'emporte

Jean

. . . on her shoulders in a sack

La Biche au Bois! Round the World in Eighty Days!
The first shows, and the first excitement! Later on,
when we know the backstage world, the actors and
the directors, when work and newspapers bring us
into contact with the theatre, we can no longer be
members of the audience. We think we are. But it is
all over. Never will the lament of the dying Tristan,
as he looks out to sea, replace in our hearts the words
of Phileas Fogg—"Twenty thousand bank notes for
you, Captain, if we reach Liverpool tonight!"—and
never will the décors of the Russian ballet leave us the
memory of those enchanted snow-covered scenes
when the Indian chief detached the engine from the
train.

When I produced *Parade* at the Châtelet in 1917 I
complained that there was insufficient light.

"Monsieur Colombier," I said to the chief elec-
trician, "I want the lighting you had for the Vegetable
Kingdom in *La Biche au Bois.*"

"How old were you then, Monsieur Cocteau?"

"Five."

"The lighting was the same as you have now," he
replied. "At that date the theatre did not possess one
quarter of the present equipment."

Alas, the gold on the crimson curtain and the brazier
footlights will never again scorch our sceptical childish
eyes.

I remember a lovely incredulous little girl, at the
Champs-Elysées. She despised the Punch and Judy
shows, roundabouts, hoop-la, the goats, the waffles,

. . . detached the engine from the train

the barley-sugar and the jug of liquorice water. She heard me excitedly telling the story of *Round the World in Eighty Days*. She smiled, shrugged her shoulders and shook back her plaits. She knew the play and told me that Phileas Fogg was thin. I had had the misfortune to see an understudy, and since my Phileas Fogg was fat, I tried to convince her that she had not seen the play properly and that she ought to see it again. She made fun of the serpents in the Aouda's grotto.

"It's a trick!" she repeated.

I was unhappy about this, and I am still unhappy when women watching Tarzan talk about tricks and dummy Hollywood lions. Indeed, ladies, the art is in the trick. Big-game hunting is an art, and when all is said and done, it is easier to make a lion out of a rug than to make a rug out of a lion.

I went recently to see a revival of *Round the World in Eighty Days*. The new setting followed that of the

. . . my Phileas Fogg was fat

original production. My neighbours looked at me with an odd expression. For the loud voices off-stage which reminded me of Pougaud's celebrated delivery, Passe-Partout falling down when he was knocked out by the opium pipe, the negro cook, the telegraphic S.O.S., the Sioux Indians' white skin showing between the sleeves of their pullovers and their redskin gloves, Phileas' wallet, the palm trees in the Grand Hotel of

India, the boilers which burst, the steamer which foundered and the wreck where Juve and Fantomas could take hold of each other on waves of green canvas heaved up on the stage-hands' backs, this collection of innocent wonders brought tears to my eyes. I confess that I am not ashamed of these tears. How can we tell from what depths our tears come and what wrings them from us? One evening, a few years ago at a performance of Offenbach's *Belle Hélène*, a friend pointed out to me in the darkness of a neighbouring box an old lady who was weeping. It was Cosima Wagner. Switzerland! Triebschen! Paul Rée! Nietzsche's phrase: "We shall go to watch the can-can danced in Paris"—cheerful youth, arguments, quarrels —Cosima Wagner would perhaps stoically have endured the ride of the Walkyries. She was weeping at the *March of the Kings*.

IV

THE CIRCUS

THE rue La Bruyère came out at the corner of the rue Moncey and the rue Blanche, opposite the wall of the Hôtel Sipierre and its chestnut trees. My German nursemaid knew the policeman on duty at the cab-rank; she called out to him and told him where we were going. I was convinced that this announcement would arouse his astonishment and envy, so I proudly walked ahead of my nurse, quickening my pace.

At the Faubourg St. Honoré a façade surmounted the gates of the New Circus. Footit and Chocolat straddled the triangle, their silhouettes standing out in colour, like the archers on the Temple of Aegina. I have already described the mysterious road which led me to the box-office courtroom. The judges tore our tickets in two, I closed my eyes . . . and I smelt the wonderful big smell.

Childhood is full of smells. Amongst others I remember the glue for the pictures we cut out in the sickroom, the lime trees at Maisons-Laffitte that flew into a frenzy when thunder was near, the delicious powder on the burnt-out fire-works nailed on to frames that we picked up in the grass next day, the arnica we had for our wasp stings, the mouldering paper in an old collection of the *Revue des Deux Mondes*, the canvas of the old carriage that used to take the family to Mass standing unharnessed in the cool coach-house among the untidy heap of picks, watering cans, croquet mallets and garden games (my cousin Marianne had once locked me inside this old carriage

... walked ahead of my nurse

and said, "Listen, I know everything. There are some grown-ups who go to bed in the daytime. The men are called *lapins* and the women are called *cocottes*; Uncle André is a *lapin*. If you tell anyone I'll beat you to death with a spade"). And then there was the heady smell of the manure in the farmyard and the ground

starred with white droppings where the greengages
split their heads open as they fell from the tree. Neither
can I forget the smell of the potted geraniums in the
hothouse and the dead frogs in the pool, with their
hands on their hearts like operatic tenors. Later I was
to know the smell of Marseilles which gives you hope,
ambergris exuded by the skin which makes you flush,
the scent of lilies crushed in alcoves, and opium which
proclaims the China of politeness and torture. But
none of these significant smells can eclipse the smell
of the circus, the smell of the New Circus, the wonderful big smell. Of course we knew it consisted of horse-
dung, coconut matting, stables and healthy sweat, but
it also contained some other indescribable ingredient,
some mixture that defied analysis, a mixture of ex-
pectation and joy which caught at your throat, which
became habit and hung over the performance until it
took the place of a curtain. And the deep rich manure
I remember from childhood helps me to understand
that this circus smell is a light, floating manure, a
powdery, golden manure which mounts up into the
glass dome, colours the globes of light with rainbow
hues, casts a glory over the acrobats' performance, and
falls again, a vital help to the flowering, multicoloured
clowns.

Escorted by the attendant and Fraülein Josephine, I
hardly reached the top of the little hatchway staircase
before my eyes were caught by this living dust, as it
cast a halo of sanctity round the rigging, the yards and
the orchestra suspended in the air above the huge ship
where the performers poured out to bursts of laughter,

to the music of trombones, cornets and the big drum.
The acrobats and clowns dominated the show for me.

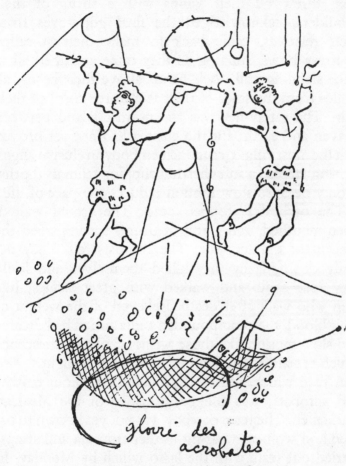

. . . casts a glory over the acrobats' performance

The rest of the programme was incidental, like the
comedians who filled in the gaps between the numbers
and helped to roll up the matting. And even better than

the turns, I preferred the acrobats when they made birdmen's gestures, dipped their shoes in the rosin box, threw off their wraps with a shrug of their shoulders, acknowledged the final good-byes from their relatives, came back to make their so-called courtesy bows, running as they came and then all at once standing still, their hands above their heads, all smiles from the soles of their feet to the roots of their hair. The safety-net was the no-man's-land between heaven and earth; for the cinema had not yet proved that the most vulgar, crude acts embody an elusive angel, a rising smoke, a soft chestnut slipping from its thorns, if only because slow motion reduces the pace of life.

The orchestra stopped dead. The crowd waited, open-mouthed, and a roll of drums accompanied the descent of the acrobats. The acrobats fell. They fell lazily down, lazily they killed themselves and lazily they rose again and walked with great strides, like men who walk after death. Relieved of the weight of their blood, they compounded a mixture of bad dreams and slow motion like those wisps of phosphorescence which remain entangled in fishing nets at night.

A turn which pleased us, in addition to our clowns and acrobats, was the performance of the Mexican marksmen. The term cowboy was not yet known to us. Men and women, wearing leather trousers and straps, carried out feats with the lasso which by Monday, in our house, ended in smashed furniture, tearful scenes and punishment in the dark cupboard.

Footit and Chocolat came on after the interval. A tiny pony trotted round the red velvet edge of the ring carrying a placard marked *"Entr'acte"* on his back. The audience rose, moved about and went to see the side-shows. The grooms in their pale blue

footit et chocolat

uniforms and brass buttons took down the parallel bars, hoisted up the trapezes and tidied away the targets, apparatus and tables used by the jugglers, marksmen and conjurors. The women selling sweets offered their *pastilles de menthe, caramels mous, bonbons acidulés*. Children turned somersaults on the coconut matting, the comedians served lemonade, and the *entr'acte* came to an end, bringing me closer to the fatal retreat, nearer to the end and the exit, when I would put my arm into the wrong sleeve of my coat as I looked despairingly towards the empty ring.

But we are not yet there. Footit and Chocolat are coming on stage. What am I saying? They would never make the mistake of coming on stage and exhibiting themselves in a music-hall. They are coming into the ring. Because the ring is not the stage. A statue cannot be a coin, and I am amazed that today's clowns are content to appear on a stage and reveal only two profiles. It looks as though the danger of not being funny, or simply danger alone, can attack from any side with the wiliness of a bull and force the stars of the circus into innumerable twists and turns like the Spaniards. The obstacle of the footlights and the orchestra pit, the man-trap of the wings and the cul-de-sac of the back-cloth are in their way. At the circus I always preferred watching these three great turns: Rastelli, Barbette and Coélano. Death has taken the one who was least concerned about her. Death remains the favourite partner of the other two. And so Barbette continues to set dubious traps for her, Coélano goes on dancing with her on the tight-rope, his eyes gazing into hers. Yes, these stars of equilibrium and the famous clowns seem to me destined for the stadium, for the ring encircled with eyes, if only by their costumes alone, which relate them to the toreadors.

Footit wore the sequins and had the suppleness, charm, fame and prestige of a toreador. He won his fame and prestige from children, the world's most difficult audience. When the ballet *Parade* was performed, I heard someone in the theatre say: "If I'd known it was so silly I'd have brought the children." This praise went straight to my heart. Footit enchanted children; he achieved at the same time the *tour de force* of pleasing the grown-ups and bringing their childhood back to them. Children are at home with the nervous excitement of clowns then they learn a new joke and decide to try it out on a friend; they understand the chief rider's scolding voice, the refusal to work, the disobedience and the grammatical mistakes. Chocolat, a stupid negro in tight black silk trousers and a red tail-coat, served as a pretext for rough jokes and blows.

Thanks to his fat bare shins, his trousers with their pompom trimmings, his starched white collar, his lock of tow-coloured hair, his harsh make-up and leering blood-red mouth, his conical hat which let fall clouds of flour when anyone hit it, his sequin-covered bodice, his crazy-duchess voice, in other words thanks to a mixture of baby, nursemaid and English great lady (his hair-style owed much to Sarah Bernhardt and Queen Alexandra), Footit brought into the ring the atmosphere of a diabolical nursery, where children could rediscover their sly malice, and where grown-ups were impressed.

The high spot of the programme was the nautical tableau. I remember with poignant regret the way the water arrived. No cinematic subterfuge or trick will ever replace that marvellous moment. Bereft of its

coconut matting, the green circus ring sank down-
wards with a dull creaking sound. Little jets of water
spurted up between the planks. As the ring became a
pool, scenery grew up around it—water-lily leaves on
which a tulle-clad dancer performed arabesques, a
transparent windmill where the rooms filled with
shadows, horses and huntsmen diving into the water,
Footit enticing a floating calf's head with oil and
vinegar, and Papa Chrysanthème's China, a panto-
mime in which Chocolat comes back from Paris
wearing a beige bowler hat and singing the fashionable
tune *Ta-ra-ra-boom de ay*.

That was the New Circus when I was seven. And
five years later, in 1904, the same New Circus was to
become the scene of an historic theatrical event: the
arrival of rhythm from America.

In 1903 the Minchin family taught us how to dance.
Madame Minchin looked like Dante and banged out
boston two-steps like *Monte-Cristo*, or *Sourire d'Avril*;
Mademoiselle Minchin might have described herself
in the line *"La Fille de Vénus et de Polichinelle"*, and
large winged dancing-pumps carried Mademoiselle's
brother over the sumptuous parquet floors at the
houses of the Godillots (we called them the prince and
princess) and Madame Fenaille.

Suddenly the cake-walk came, breaking things up
and fading the colour out of everything. Floodlights
blazed from the archways of the New Circus; silk
streamers in American colours flew from the left and
right of the doorways; the first negroes (so far we only
knew poor Chocolat) ushered in the ritual cake-walk;

a tide of elegance filled the tiered seats with women covered with pearls and feathers, men with monocles, close-cropped hair, or gleaming bald pates; the brass and drums of the orchestra attacked an unknown music, whose rhythm echoed the marches that Souza conducted and punctuated with revolver shots; the floodlights moved together like ballerinas between the double ranks of blue-clad grooms; and the Elks appeared.

Neither the first jazz at the Casino de Paris accompanying Gaby Deslys and Pilcer, nor the negro from the Black Birds in his sea-blue jacket, neither the dancer on roller skates nor the all-in wrestlers, no display of fashion and fireworks could ever be compared to this apparition.

Floodlights will not illuminate everyone. Instead they sometimes burn up some poor wretch and emphasize his solitude. Rare are those artists who gleam and flash in a glare of light. Mr. and Mrs. Elks possessed the privilege that belongs only to diamonds and stage-stars. The audience rose quivering to their feet, and in the midst of the frenzied crowd Mr. and Mrs. Elks danced, thin and bent they danced, decked with ribbons, gleaming with stars, splashed with white light, their hats over their eyes and ears, their knees higher than their backward-thrown heads, waving willowy canes in their hands, wresting the movements out of themselves and beating the artificial floor with the metal taps on their patent leather shoes.

They danced, they glided, they reared, they bent double, treble, quadruple, they stood straight again, they bowed. And behind them a whole town, the whole of Europe, began to dance. And at their example rhythm took hold of the new world and after the new world the old world, and rhythm passed into the machines and from the machines it returned to the men and could never stop again and the Elks are dead, Chocolat and Footit are dead, the New Circus is dead, and dead or alive the procession goes on dancing, led by the little canes and the ribbon-decked skeletons of the Elks.

THE SKATING RINK

ONCE upon a time two little girls in Montmartre used to dream about the Palais de Glace. They had read advertisements about it on the back page of the newspaper and the magic name stirred their imagination. This temple of winter sports had become for them a palace built of mirrors, a kind of palace of mirages. One Sunday our little girls from Montmartre broke open the money box, and, blushing with shame, in spite of their daisy-trimmed straw hats and their tarlatan dresses, found the courage to buy tickets at the entrance and cross the threshold. What a disaster! Rooted to the spot they looked at each other, divided between tears and the giggles of little girls who "can go out without their nanny". By this I mean that they were the first to laugh at their own mistake. But the effect produced was far from reciprocal. If the Palais de Glace did not impress them, they impressed the Palais de Glace, for these rash young girls were none other than Madeleine Carlier and her sister. (They had not adopted this name yet.) In that world, accustomed to the same figures circling round like the rabbit, the palm-tree and the tin soldier at the fair-ground rifle range, you can imagine the theatrical success of these new stars, these natural complexions, these four burning cheeks brightened by the pink lights, the embarrassment and the contrast between the heat of the surrounds and the strange coolness of the centre.

When the little girls found the strength to pull themselves together, take flight and end the escapade, it was with an adoring escort, an ecstatic following which in future they were never to be without.

My small self, too, thought the diadem of illuminated red letters glamorous which crowned the Palais de Glace. I gazed at this circus from our childish world, as I sat astride the wooden horses on the roundabout supported by an ivy-covered wooden bar. I made it smaller, I enlarged it, I dramatized it in my own way. But not in the same way as the little Carlier girls. I knew what to expect of it, and the prospect of skating lessons took all the poetry out of it for me in advance. For a pure-bred dunce like me, the fear of a lesson ruined my dream; the fairytale of Christmas was ruined for me by useful presents; rulers, penboxes, satchels, metronomes—objects of hatred and study.

My brother Paul skated at the Pôle Nord. The Pôle Nord in the rue de Clichy (now the Apollo), was bigger and cheaper. I filled it with ice-bergs, polar bears and sailing brigs in distress. But its sign, which lent itself to day dreams, did not distract me from the Palais de Glace because the Concorde district, the green copper roof of the Madeleine, the desert island of Madame Hédiard, queen of spices, essences and exciting fruits, the flower-market concealed behind its red cotton blinds, the phantom club terrace where leant Swann and the Duc de Guermantes, the Seine which as Apollinaire said flows between books, the pink chestnut trees in the park where indiscreet iron chairs keep the attitude of loving couples, the Guignol Anatole and the earnest butterfly hunters at the Stamp Market—this district clung to the skin of my soul and without my trying to understand why, it does so still.

"Stick at it," my brother's teacher told him, and skimmed away towards the pretty girls. This name "Stickatit" stuck to my brother and annoyed him, and gave me everything to fear concerning our first encounters on the ice.

In short, it was at the Palais de Glace in the Champs-Elysées, the real one, that my Lecomte cousins and I made our modest début. I do not think that the surroundings change much. The huge peppermint cream, covered with icy sawdust by the braking of the experts who rush along, bent double, holding their cigarettes behind their backs, and who all at once turn round completely, upright and casual, against the edge of the rink, causing a lady spectator to utter little cries, the orchestra shaking the tambourines in *España*, completing the downstrokes and upstrokes of the slow waltzes with a church-like resonance, the white powder covering the orchestra with silver, just as the airy manure of the New Circus gilded the groups of acrobats—no, apart from the tunes in fashion, it seems to me that the sky-blue plush round the draped mirrors, the rosettes and canopies of the surrounds, the light ironwork of the alcazars round the little alcoves, the slender columns and the arcades, must still be more or less the same.

Just as the New Circus befeathered itself, as though

j'ai vu, moi qui vous parle ...

... It was no small affair

by magic, with jets of water at five o'clock and changed
its style, so the Palais de Glace at five o'clock was
suddenly empty of schoolboys, girl cousins and family
parties, who gave way to the fine ladies of the fashionable world. This was the hour of the *grandes cocottes*,
who exist no more, and the *demi-castors,* persons who
would now be elegant middle-class ladies and whose
dead ranks create an enigma for us out of Madeleine

Lély in the play *Amants*, forcing André Brulé to introduce completely new tricks into his acting.

I have seen, with my own eyes, Otéro and Cavalieri lunching at Armenonville. It was no small affair. Armour, escutcheons, carcans, corsets, whalebones, braids, epaulieres, greaves, thighpieces, gauntlets, corselets, pearl baldricks, feather bucklers, satin, velvet and bejewelled halters, coats of mail—these

. . . an expensive undertaking

knights-at-arms bristling with tulle, rays of light and eyelashes, these sacred scarabs armed with asparagus holders, these Samuraïs of sable and ermine, these cuirassiers of pleasure who were harnessed and caparisoned early in the morning by robust soubrettes, seemed incapable, as they sat stiffly opposite their hosts, of extracting anything from an oyster beyond the pearl. Confronted with one of these beauties, any of our modern gigolos would take to his heels. A monocle, gaiters, a white moustache, great age and great fortune permitted one to aspire to such a *tête-à-tête*. The idea of undressing one of these ladies was an expensive undertaking which was better arranged in advance, like moving house, and before we can picture them in the midst of a chaos of underwear, hair and scattered limbs, we must intensify our powers of imagination to visualize a scandalous scene of murder.

I would like to describe one of those tables with its snow-white cloth round which hovered a *maître d'hôtel* with the whiskers of an admiral. Only the champagne bottle wore its napkin round its neck in the French style, and everything else was correct, so correct that a faint smile rewarded Boldi, the red tzigane covered with the black signature of braid, when he finished playing *Amoureuse*, on a violin surrounded by moustache.

Back in the Palais de Glace, braid adorned the olive-green uniforms of the instructors who wore caviare toques and milliners' boots. They waltzed. The *cocottes* were called Liane this, Liane that; all the lianas wound themselves round the olive green

Les tziganes

. . . a violin surrounded by moustache

instructor. Lowering their muffs they launched out, they turned, bent and rose again, imitating the noble curves of the métro entrances, and lowering their eyes, they crossed the rink. During the intervals, their silver

skates secured to their Louis XV heels, they limped towards the cloakrooms or lay, in dry dock, round the tables.

In the cloakroom our skates were taken off and our nurses dusted us down. We hung about and pro- longed our departure as long as humanly possible. We wanted to cheat over the family session and remain present, for one moment, at the entry of the *cocottes* and the artists.

Sem would draw. Armed with a Koh-I-Noor, a

truly diabolical pencil, he would slink in and out
between the groups and take up his stand behind the
goddesses of fashion and the toffs. Sem was a ferocious
insect, ill-shaven and wrinkled, adopting, as he
pursued them, the idiosyncrasies of his victims.
Everything about him, his fingers, his round spectacles, his stub of pencil, his thin sheets of tracing

Willy — Polaire
Poly chéri et Colette au
palais de glace
Jean

paper which he crumpled up and placed one on top of
each other, his wrinkles, his drooping lock of hair, his
umbrella, his dwarf stable-boy outline, everything
seemed to shrivel up and form into a group round his

desire to bite, his whole personality tying itself into a
knotted handkerchief, trying to prevent him from
forgetting one single detail in the face he was studying.

One of these tables united Willy, Colette and her

... eyes like Portuguese oysters

bulldog. Willy had thick moustaches and a beard like
Tartarin of Tarascon, sharp eyes below heavy lids,
a loose bow tie, a top hat mounted on a cardboard
halo, and he kept his hands folded like an archbishop's
over the pommel of his cane. Beside him, our own
Colette. Not the robust Colette who gave us tasty
salads made with raw onion and did her shopping in

sandals at Hédiard's stall, but a thin, thin Colette, a sort of little fox dressed up for cycling, a fox-terrier in skirts, with a black patch of hair over one eye, drawn up towards her forehead with a bow of red ribbon.

Then there appeared a creature whose name, in these surroundings, was a masterpiece in itself: Polaire. Her flat-topped serpent-like head balanced eyes like Portuguese oysters, glistening with pearls, salt and cool darkness; her features were taut, strained and drawn to the back of her head in a black cart-horse catogan. She wore a felt hat tilted backwards over her fringe, a Lalique ring in guise of a belt, and a short skirt revealing socks and button-boots with their cruel skates. She was as violent as a Yiddish insult and stood at the edge of the rink poised like a fit of hysterics.

A child's eyes register quickly. Later on he develops the film. I can see, as though it were yesterday, this silhouette of genius perched on her skates and her Javanese buskins. It was a silhouette that dominated fashion. It baffled women. It exasperated men. Sem and Cappiello fought over this yellow profile.

VI

FASHION

I HAVE allotted myself the delicate task of never violating the darkness of the grave and never unwinding the sacred wrappings. On the one hand this limits me considerably; on the other it opens up vast perspectives and makes me run the risk of being picturesque and therefore unfair. For it may be tempting to reveal the silliness of fashion and the weakness of bad periods and easy to criticize the bad moments through which all extreme forms of minor beauty pass, but this would mean imitating the unpleasant attitude which makes fun of minor beauty, that Parisian attitude, that detestable good taste which militates against what Baudelaire calls "the most recent expression of beauty". Let us not forget that *Pelléas et Mélisande,* and the canvases of Renoir and Cézanne flourished alongside the slow waltzes and romantic airs of Delmet, the Salon where every year brought back the same Didier-Pouget moorland, the same Chabas bathers, the same cardinals sitting at table playing with the cats of X, Y and Z, the same Bail peasant women who from beneath their white coiffes watched gleaming copper pans and a huge jar of gherkins reflecting a little round window, the same military allegories by Detaille, and the same busts of ministers, in marble, with iron pince-nez.

Neither must we forget that the frivolous beauty of fashion and its refinements can inspire genuine beauty or draw inspiration from it, and it can produce marvels which remain marvels, although they arouse only

Le concours Hippique

laughter in those who tolerate fashion without understanding its tragic law. Fashion dies young, and this air of being condemned endows it with nobility. It can only rely on justice late in the day, on cases won on appeal or out of remorse. Fashion must convince at the very moment it expresses itself. I have seen women entering restaurants who are enhanced by the orchestra. Such masterpieces of poise and dress sweep away our hidden treasures, spatter them with a mud of light and leave our worst bravado in the shade.

Sem told me one day that Madame Letellier, as she came to the door of the Ritz, warned the men in evening dress who formed her escort not to appear too astonished if they heard her talking gibberish, laughing and improvising a type of vocal commotion, like the large brush-strokes of a scene painter. From a distance this murmur sounded like the easy continuation of a gay, brilliant conversation and helped her to conquer stage fright, making her entry on to the stage easier, and allowing her to take it in her stride.

"My profession exhausts me," Sem went on. "What can you do? Women achieve miracles of nervous tension. They keep it up for hours on end. If I want to be there when they let go and confess their real face, I have to stay on the lookout until four or five o'clock in the morning."

These bitter words are food for thought. It is indeed a tempting moment when the marvels of fashion give way to new ones and reveal their own absurdity. But it can happen that they are only absurd for a short time. With a little patience anyone who likes liking people and detests the easy vivacity of insult, may have surprises. The woman who gives up and lets go, abandoning the mincing faces of the struggle, becomes a very beautiful old lady, the old styles blossom out in serenity and can be seen outside the convention of fashion.

Of course the hieratic thistles in embossed leather

and the acrid pokerwork irises of our childhood came
to the same end as the raspberries of Madeleine
Lemaire and the peonies that my sister Marthe painted

at the watercolour class, chewing her brush and recit-
ing the tirades of Cyrano de Bergerac.

It would be easy for me to remind you of the Helleu
etching which adorned young girls' bedrooms, with
their white-painted furniture—a lady standing by her
sunshade with her head in the air, like those Maupas-
sant heroines standing by the rails of a ship (with

seagulls on their hats, seagulls on the waves, seagulls everywhere), the black Aiglon cape with its high silver-fringed collar, and my mother's cold astrakhan

bolero, as curly as a faithful poodle, in which I used to bury my face, breathing in the perfumed dampness that she brought back from her morning walk.

FASHION

Mountains breathe, move, slide against one another, climb up and penetrate into each other, and the century-long slowness of this rhythm escapes us, revealing a static spectacle. The cinema has shown us that plants gesticulate and that only a difference in tempo between the animal and vegetable kingdoms led us to believe in the serenity of nature. We must change our minds; we climb down, now that those admirable fast-motion films have let us into the secret of a rose, the birth of a bean or the explosion of a crocus.

A similar film should be made of the slow-moving periods and fashions that succeed one another. Then it would be really exciting to see at high speed dresses growing longer, shorter and longer again; sleeves growing fuller, tighter, then full again; hats going down and up, perching on top, lying down flat, becoming decorative then plain; bosoms growing fuller then slighter, provocative and ashamed; waists changing places between breasts and knees; the ocean-swell of hips and haunches; stomachs which advance and retreat; petticoats which cling and froth; underwear which disappears and reappears; cheeks which go hollow then full, then paler and redder and pale again; hair which grows longer, disappears, grows again, becomes curly, smooth or frizzy, grows out or stands on end, twists and then untwists, bristles with combs and pins, abandons them and takes them up again; shoes which hide the toes and then lay them bare; braids knotted over prickly woollens. And silk conquers wool, wool conquers silk; tulle floats, velvet hangs heavy, sequins sparkle, satins crease, furs slip over dresses and around necks, going up and down and round the edges, and curling up in frenzied panic like the animals from whom they are taken.

Then we would see the frivolous accessories of the period when we grew up live with an intense life, assuming only graceful postures, and we could watch the superb, seething spectacle of a true Medusa's head which tells us more about a certain style than the under ground arches or the Lalique medallions.

Faute de mieux, since this experiment still belongs, alas, to the realm of imagination, I advise you to go and look again at the Lalique jewellery whenever it is exhibited. You will be astonished by the cocks holding amethysts in their beaks, the cornflowers entwined together, the snakes twisted round each other, the enamel and precious stones, and the ingenious flora and fauna. You will be a little ashamed of the sober invisible mounts. A goldsmith indicates his period with the flourish of the inimitable signature on a banknote. (Shall I reveal to you that Paul Iribe is at the origin of these knotted snakes? As a young artist working for Lalique he copied for his employer the snakes that he carried about in his sleeves and pockets.)

Another marvel was one of Sarah Bernhardt's coiffures, made of iron and turquoise flowers and exhibited by Sacha Guitry in the foyer of the Théâtre de la Madeleine, next to the enormous tiny shoes of Little Titch.

This is already enough to prevent us from laughing too heartily at the Modern Style and enough to give us fears about our own disgust when we come to examine the styles of today.

Every play mysteriously retains the imprint of the type of language peculiar to that brief period when it was written and acted. At the Comédie Française the repeated "mademoiselles" in *La Voix Humaine* are beginning to sound like the "madames" in the tragedies of Racine. I accept this and I shall not replace the telephone girls by an automatic exchange. In fact the complications caused by the telephone during this period are things of the past.

If a play is revived only five years after its first production I believe that the actors should be made to accept the fashions current at its creation. If the play survives, these fashions become costumes[1] and the playwright wins the round.

---

[1] It is the dress designer's problem to suppress what is ridiculous in the clothes of the last period and emphasize their charm. Make no mistake, even a singer who wears costumes should make them undergo transformations. There are Carmens and Manons of 1900, 1929 and 1935. Why not something of 1930 in 1935? There would be no more laughter to fear and the eye would enjoy this indispensable difference between the audience and the stage.

VII

SCHOOL

IN these surface recollections it is impossible for me to pass over my schooldays in silence—to my great shame. For I was the typical bad scholar, incapable of learning or remembering anything whatsoever. My prizes for gymnastics, German and drawing only gave an extraordinary emphasis to my bad conduct and framed it, so to speak, with gold. If I close my eyes, my memories of school are void and gloomy: waking to the threat of punishment; tears, dirty exercise books, books hastily opened, ink blots, raps over the knuckles with a ruler, the squeak of chalk, Sunday detentions, empty classrooms stinking of gas, little prison tables at which I copied out a thousand times "eight plus eight does not make fourteen" in handwriting as flabby as the shape of a fishknife; suburbs, miserable departures and homecomings, autumn trains where the big boys tied us up with string and threw us up into the luggage rack. I could describe other tortures: dormitories at dawn, the mortal agony of being questioned, attempts to copy from my neighbour who surrounded himself with a wall of dictionaries, floods of threats, the discovery of obscene caricatures, cold sweats until I was delivered by the beating of the drum which caused a cheerful uproar and unwound my heart. My poor family despaired and tried everything. The Petit Condorcet, the Grand Condorcet, the Cours Fénelon and private tutors at home! But what can be done when a child's heart is empty, when he is reserving himself for secret tasks, trying to sleep like a somnambulist, and well-meaning murderers wake him sharply at the very edge of his dreams?

My real memories of school began when the exercise books were closed. Even the recreation ground was subjected to the cold shadow and the guillotine-blade of the blackboard. Tricks, fights, escapades, playing truant in the rue Blanche and the passage du Havre are what I, the dunce, remember, and it is this that I, the bad scholar and the free man, have retained in my memory.

Crommelinck made a play out of my book *Les Enfants Terribles*. This unpublished play was to be performed at the Théâtre de l'Œuvre. The battle-ground of my childhood, its hall of miracles, especially when it was idealized by snow and softened with fairytale, was the Cité Monthiers, where you enter the Théâtre de l'Œuvre by a gate from the rue de Clichy and where our army of knights in woollen armour, carrying satchel-bucklers, invaded at a gallop, between four and five in the afternoon, through the archway of a building in the rue d'Amsterdam opposite the doors of the Petit Condorcet.

Like Maeterlinck at Saint-Wandrille, we could have asked the audience to leave the theatre and make them watch the prologue, the snowfight, at the very scene of the crime.

I will not undertake another description of the Cité

79

La vrai cité monthier

Jean

. . . battleground of my childhood

Monthiers in the snow, or, to be precise, in the gleaming mud and grey snow which I tried to reproduce in my film *Le Sang d'un Poète* and which led the admirers of Russian films to believe that we had economized with cotton wool and bicarbonate of soda. It is true that the snow remained unblemished on the cornices and gas lamps and on the zinc shutters of the private houses that looked on to this miniature city, which I am always led to describe and draw larger than life by my tendency to mythologize and enlarge receding events. The flickering gaslight added a touch of villainy. The shadowy corners grew deeper, the houses grew fiercer, the pale soft snow achieved the rest. And now that I am trying to be exact, here I am losing my foothold and at the slightest excuse I could embark on some unimaginable story as a marginal note to the first chapter of *Les Enfants Terribles*.

In actual fact something like the snowball story did happen. One of my friends did fall down dead, and I suspect that the oceans of blood that he coughs up in my film must, by the same mechanism which leads painters to make the mount of Golgotha and the cross of Christ higher and higher, come down to a very small quantity of blood flowing from one nostril, the trickle of congealed blood on the nose of a dead hare. But the fatal snowball was certainly thrown at him by Dargelos.

I must tell you about Dargelos, for he is the symbol of the magnificent duffer, just as Clinchard was the

symbol, in our small classes, of the swot. One day we saw Clinchard's mother hit him, in the presence of our mother, in the vestibule. Our hearts filled with hope when we learned that his mother had punished him because he was second. He had the first place, once and for all, and he had to stick to it.

Dargelos occupied once and for all the last place, the first place among the duffers. But he occupied it with such force, daring and calm that none of us would have thought of taking it away from him, or even of envying him. Need I add that he possessed beauty, the beauty of an animal, a tree or a river, that insolent beauty which is emphasized by dirt, which seems to be unaware of itself, takes advantage of the slightest resource it possesses and only needs to appear in order to convince. This sturdy, sly, obvious beauty bewitched the people who were least likely to be influenced by it: the provost, the vice-principal, the teachers, the assistants, the ushers, the porter. Imagine the havoc that could be created by Dargelos—gang-leader and cock of the walk, the duffer who went unpunished, Dargelos with his night-black lock of hair, his half-closed eyes and bruised proud knees—on grubs like us, desperate for love, unaware of the enigma of the senses and possessing the least protection in the world against that terrible damage caused to every sensitive heart by the supernatural sexuality of beauty.

I have always supposed that Dargelos was aware of his privilege and made use of it. He was the school vamp. He astonished us, crushed us, spattered us with his moral luxury and developed in us that celebrated inferiority complex which is certainly far too much talked of but exists all the same and, more so than pride, is the cause of much misery.

Dargelos despised us as a whole. To win a favour from him gave rise to intrigues worthy of the memoir writers of Versailles.

... He was the school vamp

I have spoken of the "scene of the crime". Was a crime committed? After *Les Enfants Terribles* I have so often read and heard that the snowball thrown by Dargelos contained a stone that finally I have almost convinced myself of it. But the stone was useless. I have always believed that mere contact with Dargelos would have been enough to change the snow into marble and harden it into murder, and that in his hands it would become as dangerous as a Spanish knife. This snowball, the origin of a scandal which finally formed the thread of my book, gleams with a phosphorescent light. It struck Paul's chest like a blow

from a statue. Afterwards the statue became still and nobody thought of accusing it. Dargelos wiped his hands on his woollen cape, tossed his muffler back over his shoulder, dismissed his staff officers, put his tongue out slightly between his teeth, winked with one eye, picked up his black leather bag and (abandoning his victim) ran away through the rue d'Amsterdam.

If I dwell on this it is because this episode illuminates to a wonderful extent how memories are formed and deformed.

Now that Dargelos has left my intimate Olympus, like the gipsy violinist who leaves the orchestra and goes to play among the tables, he spells dream for many unknown young readers. I have not changed his name. Dargelos was Dargelos. This name is identified with arrogance. Where does he live? Is he alive? Will he appear? Will his ironic ghost appear to me, carrying my book?

Perhaps I shall have the great surprise of finding a humble, hardworking and retiring Dargelos, stripped of his fable, regretting, through me, what eventually he would regard to be faults, and perhaps succeeding in overcoming them. Perhaps he will ask me to give him back his power and the secrets of his prestige. I would prefer him to remain in the shadow for which I have substituted his constellation, and for him to remain for me the example of everything which cannot be learnt, taught, judged, analysed and punished, everything that makes a person individual, the first symbol of the untamed forces that dwell within us, which the social machine tries to kill and which motivate, beyond good or evil, those individuals whose example consoles us for the fact of living.

VIII

1900

CHILDREN go through life in a state of half-sleep. Fraülein Josephine used to stretch me out on her knees as I curled up under the table napkin and digested my soup. How delightful it was, from under my napkin, in the half-sleep of childhood, to listen to her eating. The jaw sound and the stomach sound, the crumbs falling, the heartbreaking sighs uttered by governesses whose *responsibilities overwhelm them,* the entire drama of a dinner below-stairs, accompanied by eyes turned heavenwards and little fingers extended, reached me muffled by the table-linen and the edges of dream.

Linen and shawls and plaids and capes. . . . Streets that one crossed on the way to see the magic lantern at a neighbour's house, the forest of Saint-Germain by dark, other nights with steamboats and Swiss funicular railways, lakes gleaming far away, far below; and, far up, walls of ice which breathed, waterfalls which thundered, hotels which smelt of wooden floors; customs inspections, strange music made by the roof and wheels of a railway carriage. Thus it was, as children cross the big world between their mother's arms and the embrace of dreams, that later on I reconstructed incidents to suit myself.

Santos-Dumont manœuvres his propeller; from a

Santos . Dumont

... waves an American flag

small straw basket, beneath a flying cigar, he waves an American flag. In full flight Sem sketches the aeronaut's clipped moustache, his hollow cheeks and his flabby neck with its butterfly bow.

Standing between two municipal guards Madame Humbert, her eyes like drills beneath her otter fur toque, exploits the Crawford fortune, makes ministers commit suicide and amuses the crowd. The Bazar de la Charité! The streets full of cries, and a funereal carnival of red fire-engines, with their bellies low on the ground, red ladders and men with golden helmets like allegorical figures, a rain of sparks, and soot which turns into crêpe and descends over all the noble families of France. The luck of not being old enough to understand the Dreyfus affair. The "kikes", the *Psst*, which was the newspaper of Forain and Caran D'Ache, the anti-Dreyfusards at Maisons-Lafitte who after dinner crept past the gates covered with ivy, wisterias and honeysuckle, trying to catch the Dreyfusards unawares. *L'Assiette au Beurre* where Caran d'Ache's pen immortalized Kruger's horseshoe beard. The Adelward-Fersen affair. . . . Schoolboys picked up at the school gates to attend black masses, wearing garlands of roses on their heads. The trial of the German princes and the newspapers that were hidden and the conversations that broke off as soon as we came in. The visit of the Tsar and Tsarina, the Pont Alexandre, the coach and four with two postilions behind the theatrical trotting of Montjarret, Felix Faure's outrider, the Russian national anthem flowing like Moscow, Edmond Rostand's poem: *Oh! oh! c'est une impératrice!* recited at

Compiègne by Madame Bartet dressed as a nymph
and parodied by Eve Lavallière. The universal exhibi-
tion which left me memories vaguer than any theatrical
memory which precedes it.

Out of this confused and dusty circus I have retained
one solitary vital luminous image: Madame Loïe
Fuller. Nothing remains of the Guillaume troupe, of
Cléo de Mérode in her golden cuirass, the escalator,
the *maréoramas, stéréoramas,* the castle upside down and
the illuminated fountains. But is it possible on the
contrary to forget the woman who discovered the
dance of the age? A large American woman, rather
ugly and bespectacled, standing on a transparent
trap-door, uses rods to manœuvre oceans of light
veiling, and sober, active and invisible like a hornet in
a flower, she stirs up an orchid of light and fabric
which billows out, flares up, opens, roars, turns and
floats, changing shape like clay in a potter's hands,
twisted in the air under the sign of the torch and the
hair. Maxim's, the Grand Palais, Lalique—yes, they
can give you some idea of 1900, they are the burnt-out
fireworks. Let us salute the dancer who lit the fireworks, who touched off this ghost, an epoch where
woman (with her petticoats and her undulating grace)
reigns to the extent of occupying the place on the
marble horses of the Grand Palais that is usually
reserved for young men.

The Parisienne dominates the century, on the giant
gate of the Place de la Concorde, and everywhere, in
music, painting, poetry, the theatre, and furniture, the
froth of her many-layered skirts will enshroud angles

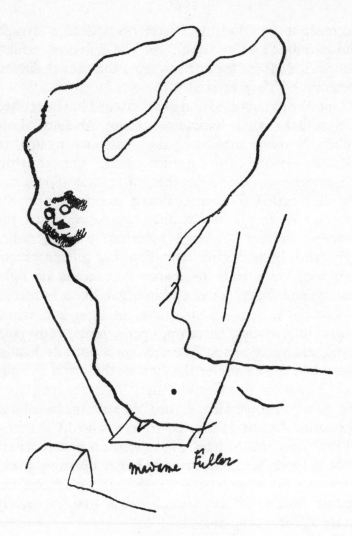

madame Fuller

. . . A large American woman

and lines until negro art, sport, Picasso and Chanel sweep away this muslin mist and force the triumphant woman either to return to her place in the home or to adopt the rhythm of the stronger sex. It is true that the cinema will soon give her back her rights and will allow her to aspire to the aggressive role of being a work of art. I mean that here she will find arguments against unrewarding domestic toil and in two magnificent manifestations, Greta Garbo and Marlene Dietrich, she will find the example of an ideal which consists of taking a hair from the dog that bit her and repolishing the weapons of sex-appeal against men.

Let us return to the period of my last chapter. After being expelled from the Grand Condorcet for bad conduct, I worked for my *baccalauréat* with M. Dietz. I cannot rival André Gide's description of this master who astonished us by the contrast between his protestantism and his odalisque poses. He spread himself out, sank down, tied himself into knots, untied himself, stretched one arm in one direction, and a leg in the other, watching us over his pince-nez, shaking with ironic laughter.

Our Condorcet escapades in the rue Caumartin led us to the Looping the Loop (the former Pôle Nord) where fashion demanded that we looped our loop in a speed car. We met there a young person who used to haunt our nights: Alice de Pibrac. She introduced one of her girl-friends to us, a blonde who claimed that she had a part in a five-act play with Sarah Bernhardt. "Sarah," she said in between two loops, "has a hump back. In the end she throws away her hump and marries me." We thought she was lying, but were wrong. She was called Lilian Greuse and the play was *Les Bouffons* by Zamacoïs.

. . . cold and damp bombardment

Our love of the theatre found something to feed on at M. Dietz's establishment in the rue Claude Bernard. His son acted at the Comédie-Française under the pseudonym of Garry and his nephew Pierre Laudenbach was preparing to become Pierre Fresnay. On Sundays and Thursdays I rushed off to join my accomplices René Rocher and Carlito Bouland (a friend who found the courage in his likeness to Coquelin to learn by heart all the tirades in his repertoire); we pooled our money and for a moderate sum we took the *avant-scène* box No. 2 at the Eldorado. I forget to add that we took with us a basket full of bunches of violets with which we bombarded the singers—a juvenile, clumsy, cold and damp bombardment which left them divided between smiles and anger. This *avant-scène* box did not consider itself unimportant. It even formed part of the show by reason of its location halfway between the footlights and the spotlights. I think its moderate price was due to its inconvenience, for the only visible part of the stage was concealed between the scrolls of the double basses and the heads of the cellists who played standing up. But the essential thing was the proscenium where the artists appeared. Against the light the audience seethed behind a zone of luminous dust. We could see no further than the pale blue plush edge of our box and the conductor of the orchestra, Monsieur Dédé, a crinkly-haired moustachioed negro, who wore spectacles and conducted in white gloves.

I pity the young people of today who have only ghosts to wait for when the film is over. Our group adored Mistinguett, the princess of the Eldo, and we used to wait for her at the stage door in the Faubourg Saint-Martin.

In actual fact our loves were reduced to the level of our means. Number One on the programme, Jeanne Reynette, was my delight. If school had been a theatre

programme, I would always have had the same
honours as an American star. Alas, just as I was
bottom of the class, so Reynette was bottm of the
bill, and this particular fact made us worthy of

Reynette
(le N°
1)

Jean

each other. She wore a short skirt and little socks,
carried a cane and had knees less noble but just as
battered as Dargelos; she also had the pleasant quality
of laughing at her own wrong notes. This laughter
amused the audience and won sympathy for her. What

became of her, you will ask? I can tell you, for one day the former Spanish ambassador astonished me with a detailed description of our box, which he had heard from Reynette, who had come into wealth and was now a grand lady of Montevideo.

I will pass over the girls my friends admired—Angèle Moreau, an opulent gigolette who wore a red scarf, and Mary Hett, who had barbed-wire eyelashes, a hint of moustache and roguish beauty-spots. Now I come to the star of the place. Dranem had just sung: "*Ah! les p'tits pois, les p'tits pois, les p'tits pois*" and "*Pétronille tu sens la menthe*", with his eye down on his cheek and his hat down on his eye. The orchestra attacked the Matchiche and then, beneath the hail of our bouquets, her hands on her hips, her sombrero ready for the fray, a Spanish shawl draped over her short skirt, Mistinguett made her entry. After the Matchiche and "*Femme torpille, pille, pille—qui se tortille, tille, tille*", she left the stage beneath a new salvo of bouquets. Then began the panic and the drawing of lots to decide which one of us would go to see her, braving the stage doorkeeper at the end of a sinister cul-de-sac. The meetings with our singing stars took place at the Taverne Pschorr. But no true romance could compete with our one-minute discussion with Mistinguett near the doorkeeper's box, as she held her flowered wrapper over her bosom and surprised us with her "bicycles", the make-up she always used, which consisted of drawing the spokes of a wheel in blue pencil to imitate the shadow of the eyelashes between her eyebrows and the rim of her eyes.

Many years afterwards, at the home of her son, my very dear friend Léopold, I was looking at the family album. First of all I saw an ageless woman, who

. . . his eye down on his cheek and his hat down on his eye

seemed to be more or less a peasant, holding a baby. "My mother," said Léopold. Then with each photograph the peasant woman grew younger and won the race. The album was the reverse of the usual middle-class variety, for his mother, becoming younger and younger and more and more elegant, brought the celebrated figure of Mistinguett to perfection, with her big cheerful mouth, her animal-like eyes which never smiled, her chestnut curls and her silken legs.

Mistinguett once asked her sister-in-law to telephone me, saying that she would be glad if I came to see her revue. At the Folies-Bergère she had reserved for me the box which corresponded to the avant-scène No. 2. It was therefore from the same youthful angle that I saw her emerge from a forest of ostrich feathers, simply dressed in a tailored suit, without jewellery; she walked forward to the audience, and there, going beyond the footlights, looking at every part of the house, she sang the song: *"Oui. C'est moi, me voilà, je m'ramène."*

There are several types of patriotism. I try to thicken that skin which in everyone is sensitive to military marches, but why should I thicken that deep-lying skin which makes Mistinguett's voice unbearable to me when I am away and makes me listen to her as a Scot hears the bagpipes, a Spaniard the castanets and a Pole the piano? She may sing the lament of a poor child standing by a big dog, like the young aristocrats of Velasquez, or she may explain to the audience: *"On dit que j'ai la voix qui traîne—Quand je chant' mes rengaines—c'est vrai."* Tears come into my eyes when I hear this voice that has studied so long in the school of street cries and newspaper sellers, this voice made for laments, this voice which is one more expression of

that face which was built out of blows on the head.

During the interval I took into her dressing-room one of the most beautiful young women of our day. Hardly had they been introduced and hardly had the young woman sat down before a phenomenon occurred; beauty and youth were extinguished by this woman who would soon be taking part in a snow scene, wearing a long fiery dress and eclipsing the very young gigolos who escorted her. "Come," one of my women readers will say to me, "you speak of Mistinguett as though she were Duse. What part can she play? What playwright can she interpret? Who are her heroines?" I do not know. She incarnates herself. She expresses what is best in my town. She appeals to the patriotism of which I am not ashamed. Above all I respect this burning desire to shine with the light that takes so long to reach mankind and belongs by right to the stars.

IX

VILLEFRANCHE

TONIGHT I am writing this chapter at the Hôtel Welcome at Villefranche-sur-Mer. This hotel is a source of myths, a place that young people enamoured of lyricism should transform into an altar and deck with flowers. Poets of every sort and every language have lived there and by mere contact between their emanations have transformed this extraordinary little town, whose precipitous untidiness stops at the edge of the water, into a real Lourdes, a centre of fable and invention. The world was at the mercy of cubes, corrugated iron and crystal; Christian Bérard fought back with an airy capharnaum originating, one could guess, in this old-fashioned Nice, city of stories, carnival, cavalcades and battles of flowers, city of plaster and gold, a city you walk through in a dream, astonished by the sordid luxury, the red squares, flower beds, arches, *trompe l'œil* and the crowds who climb on white chairs to applaud the procession of the waves. Statues standing on one leg at roof-corners, fiacres with parasols, Chinese shops, English invalids, Russian families, children fighting, Pierrots dancing farandoles. I suppose that no Italian comedy décor is more likely to haunt the waking sleep of poets than this conjuror's theatre for which the little town of Villefranche seems to form the wings. Yes, from

Villefranche, from the Hôtel Welcome with its pale blue rooms looking on to the golf course and the American or British fleet, its oriflammes, Shakespearean fanfares, jazz bands and hymns, Christian Bérard showed young people the wax faces, the listening heads behind red draperies, women with their fingers at their lips beside sleeping figures, bakers from garrisons of moonlight, men who stole children, little girls who put out their tongues behind study doors, the infirm denizens of heaven and the other wonders which peopled your solitude in 1935 and would never have done so without our gay company and without the hotel with the graceful marble and iron balconies.

How silent it is tonight! The town is still, the sea is still and invisible, the boats, so full of light, are still, and seem to lie a little above the level of the sea, the buoys are still, the lighthouse sends its megaphone beams over the hills and a few crickets imitate the discourse of the stars. Four years of a desire to live and work miracles, four long years have piled up between the Villefranche where I am writing these lines and the Villefranche where we used to live, where I wrote *Orphée* and the poems of *Opéra*, where I took the Montboron road on my way back from the Stravinskys', my ears still glowing with the golden, curling, twisting, beringed music of *Oedipus Rex*.

And tonight, in front of my open window which frames the dialogue of the lighthouse and the red harbour light and the moon, so clear that it would be naïve to see anything in it except a ruin, and this dead water, and these boats resting on nothingness, I think I am not sitting at my table to write a description or to complain, and this book belongs to a past which is much less new. Indeed the past is only the future grown old and the present is the past still young. Past, present and future only exist by a trick of folding which allows us to make an external and quite accidental contact with eternity, where the interior design, like the paper lace cut out by conjurors' scissors, must be of a heart-breaking monotony. It remains true none the less that I have set myself a programme and I hope to stick to it: to recount, gradually, anywhere, not what interests only a few people but what may interest a great number. I mean that instead of writing my memoirs I will appeal to my memory and stimulate it, then wait for what will come out of it, and, thanks to a sort of conducted liberty, or half-sleep, see this face or that landscape come to life, issuing from my pen like ectoplasm from the mouth of a medium. And tonight, when I force it out by the intervention of these memories of Villefranche and the guests who made a dream kitchen of it, tonight an unexpected face materializes, a sphinx standing at the door which leads from childhood to adolescence, a door which too often, alas, through the blindness of families, leaves only the memory of the upholstered entrance to a place of ill-repute.

In September, 1931, I had typhoid fever at Toulon. Toulon, where I was living side by side with a monkey and an Annamite boy, is an affecting town, the real Toulon of *Consolata, Daughter of the Sun*, as long as one's health remains good. It is less amusing to be ill there, when the boy loses his head and the monkey tries to bite and the hotels turn you out. The doctor and the nursing home, Jean Desbordes and the Bourdets were my guardian angels. Denise and Edouard Bourdet came to see me every day, and I read *La Prisonnière*, which I was only to see when it was revived. Fever gives you second sight. Thanks to two lines spoken by the young woman: "She knows everything", "She never lies", and to a sentence spoken by Madame d'Aiguines' husband, a face I knew imperiously took the place of the character whom Bourdet leaves in the background, like the Arlésienne and some of Maeterlinck's heroes. It was like a face drawn in invisible ink. Hold it in front of the fire and the white sheet of paper reveals its secret. And indeed this face and afterwards the figure of the woman lying on her bed came out of the darkness of my memory by the light of a winter fire, among the crêpes de Chine and the furs.

I asked Bourdet if the model for the woman who haunts the play by her absence was really Madame X. It was. Since he was surprised that when I was a school-boy I had known a woman who saw practically no-body, I told him about the reason for our first meeting, the friendship that was to follow and the mark that this friendship was to leave on me for ever.

At M. Dietz's establishment we were all intrigued

by one of the very young pupils. He had a big head like a kind-hearted ogre and exuded charm from his mouth with its countless teeth, his shaggy hair and his haunted eyes the colour of purple ink. We could feel that he was surrounded with luxury yet alone, in spite of swift-moving doctors in sable pelisses, and a tutor—almost a warder—who forced him to write down his dreams. He died of meningitis. He had been taken home. His mother asked if I would come to see her and we arranged to meet one Sunday, late in the afternoon.

You must understand what my life was like. I knew nothing and, what is more, there was no sign at that time of a type of interior decoration which is widespread today.

I knew the rue La Bruyère, with its ivory and ebony tables, the dining-room chairs with chocolate-brown initials on a coffee-coloured background, the extending dining-room table, the drawing-room dominated by the bronze statue of Dante, the small drawing-room with the stork lamp and the upright piano, my mother's bedroom furnished in flowered chintz, our bedrooms with their white lacquered furniture, the etchings by Helleu, the Bibliothèque Rose and Jules Verne on the bookcase where we built a shrine to the Virgin Mary and the crib at Christmas time.

I was quite unprepared therefore, and I had no idea that other décors and other milieux existed, when I went from the plush of the family notaries, bankers and admirals to the extraordinary apartment of

Madame X, who, as you will have guessed, was none other than my dead comrade's mother. Parquet floors, thick woollen rugs in black and white, rice straw across the empty partitions, Spanish furniture, eighteenth-century colonial style English armchairs, low red lacquer tables, anemones standing upright in a Chinese bowl, an old silver kakemono, a Greek marble bust, incense smouldering in a jade cup, Coromandel screens, a hammock slung from one wall to another in a small beige satin room adorned with Japanese cushions in dark purple, parchment screens—the entire style which was to spread to a tedious extent, and which you know by heart, this woman invented it and grouped it together for the first time.

Lying stretched out near a log fire she looked at me. I had expected mourning with crêpe and tears, like ours. She was smiling, and wore one of those purple Chinese cassocks which buttoned on the shoulder. Above the upright collar was a slender neck and the neck supported a delicate head belonging to the central figure in Carpeaux's picture *La Danse*, silvered or gilded in turn by her hair and the firelight. She-devil, she-clown or Bacchus, young woman or young man, with a face like Barbette when he took hold of the trapeze and jumped, my friend's mother was toasting bread by the fire, with a little golden fork.

You can imagine in what state I came home for supper. The family was at table. I barely heard the reprimand. My ears were buzzing. My heart was beating. I looked round me like a drunkard, and when I tried to describe where I had been and blurt out my secret like an insult, I realized my helplessness and my sacrilege, and in the midst of mocking laughter I shed hot tears.

La Prisonnière! When I left Madame X's flat I passed in the hallway a beautiful young woman whose colossal feet and hands, priest-like hat and velvet smoking-jacket had surprised me.

Only now can I solve the enigma of this visit, the semi-darkness, the proud solitude, the sad smile, the forbidden sweetness and this son smitten by the furious goddesses of Lesbos, isle of sterility.

X

ISADORA, SARAH AND DE MAX

EUROPE is becoming more and more a confused factory of desperation and killing. In this vast enterprise of despair there remain still a few places disguised in fancy-dress where the hours pass happily.

Villefranche, where royalty used to disembark, is one of them. In the past distant princesses were welcomed there by our ambassadors for state marriages. The smallest of its little squares could provide the décor for a Goldoni imbroglio, a Mozart opéra-bouffe, or an unkind farce by Molière.

Shadows of balustrades, palm trees and women doing their hair. . . . Over bedroom ceilings near the port wavers the reflected gleam of watered-silk, an imitation marble of living light.

Grasped between the walls of the Monte Carlo road and the fortress of Vauban, Villefranche always looks like a town the day before or after a holiday. This evening, leaning against an archway in the roofed-over town, I close my eyes and I remember the laughter that will never be laughed again, or perhaps laughed somewhere else, unknown to my generation.

Paris in 1912. Balls, balls, balls. The Baby Ball at Madame Gillou's! It was winter. It was freezing. Baron D., an old amateur actor, wearing a sailor suit from Old England, with a lace collar, bare legs, white socks, short trousers, carrying a hoop and a straw hat covered with ribbons, hurried along in his hired landau. Alas, at the corner of the Place de la Madeleine and the Boulevard Malesherbes, the horse slipped and fell down dead. Baron D. had to get out. A policeman took particulars. The scene drew a crowd. Insults and threats came from all sides, including the policeman. "Officer, I was going to the Baby Ball." "Quiet! I've heard that one before. What's your address?" The unhappy old man waved his hoop, quivering, crimson with shame. He took his papers out of a little pocket in his little trousers.

January 1st, 19—— The *Phare de Villefranche* writes: "Ball at the Hotel W. . . . Among the attractive costumes, M. de M . . . Paper Phrygian cap . . ." And among the society notes in the *Eclaireur de Nice*: "*Fête des fleurs*. The president of our pigeon-shooting and fencing clubs was very much noticed in his cart. The wheels were made of irises, the whip of wall-flowers!"

This naïve statement sums up the Nice which lasted from Marie Bashkirtseff to Isadora Duncan: the Nice where Harlequins behind iron railings bombarded each other with plaster marbles.

Isadora! Let my reverie rest a moment on her, that admirable woman worthy of these times and places which violate the rules of good taste, push them roughly aside and go beyond them. I would like to paraphrase Nietzsche and Wilde: *She has lived the best of her dance*. The details hardly mattered to her. She did not narrow her eyes like an artist, and she did not stand back. She wanted to live massively, beyond beauty and ugliness, to seize hold of life and live it face to face, eye to eye. She belonged to the school of Rodin. Here was a dancer who did not much care if

her dress slipped and revealed shapeless shapes, if her flesh trembled or if sweat ran down her. All these things lagged behind her inspiration. Asking men for children and getting them and making a success of them and losing them horribly by one stroke of savage ill-luck, dancing at the Trocadéro with the Colonne orchestra or on esplanades in Athens and Moscow with a gramophone—this Jocasta died as she lived, a victim of the complicity of a racing car and a red

Isadora débute

Jean ✱

. . . revealed shapeless shapes

scarf. A scarf which hated her, threatened her and warned her; which she braved, and obstinately went on wearing.

Our youth, when we were mad about the theatre, was dominated by two great figures: Sarah Bernhardt and Edouard de Max. It was Isadora Duncan who brought these names to my pen. How were they concerned with the done thing, with tact and balance, those princes of what is not done, those tigers who licked themselves and yawned in front of everyone, those forces of artifice who struggled against that force of nature, the public?

Mounet-Sully was declining. This old blind lion slept in a corner of the menagerie. Sometimes he dealt a masterly blow with his paw: *Oedipe-Roi*. Sarah and de Max often acted together, opposite the Châtelet where we saw *Michel Strogoff* and *Les Pilules du Diable*.

What excitement when the yellow curtain parted at the end of the play, and the tragedienne bowed, the claws of her left hand embedded in her right breast, her right hand and her straight left arm leaning on the edge of the proscenium. Like some Venetian palace she sank beneath the weight of necklaces and fatigue, painted, gilded, engineered, propped up and covered with flags, in the midst of a dovecote of applause. *La Sorcière! La Samaritaine! Phèdre! Andromaque!* . . . Hermione rests in her dressing-room. Orestes goes mad. "*Pour qui sont—ces serpents—qui sifflent—sur—vos têtes*". De Max panted, shaking his serpent-like locks and waving draperies about like Loïe Fuller. A sort of

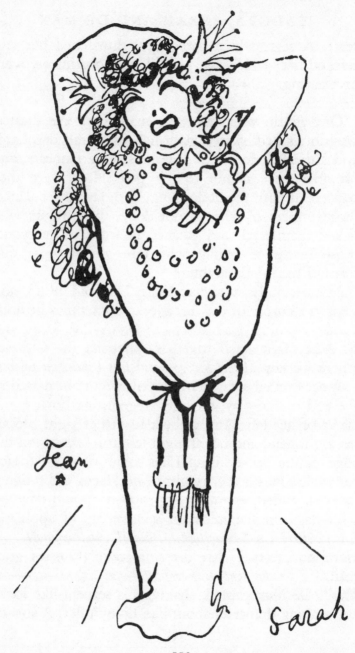

poignant lament accompanied him, which for a long time we took for some sound in the wings and was nothing more than the siren of the paddle steamer at the Châtelet landing-stage.

De Max was a tragedian of genius. Like Mesdames Duncan and Bernhardt, he was ignorant of codes and formulas. He searched and invented. He embarrassed. He went off the rails. We felt as though we were responsible for his mistakes. We did not dare look at our neighbours; we sweated hotly. Suddenly we were ashamed of being ashamed. Shouts of "quiet" suppressed the last laugh. With a raging fist de Max tamed ridicule and leapt astride it. His pride carried him away and carried us away at a gallop.

How can I forget his Néron in *Britannicus*, an operetta Néron, with an emerald monocle and a train, played in such a way that it made you unable to imagine any other?

René Rocher knew de Max. I think he rang the bell at his door in the rue Caumartin, a few yards from our school, opposite the Passage du Havre where we used to buy sneezing powder, tickling hairs and stink-bombs. De Max never sent anyone away. He admitted Rocher into his circle, and Rocher, swollen with pride, took me with him.

Like the sea, whose motion, sound and grey-green colour he possessed, de Max's name spelt terror to any mother. (Except mine, who trusted me and was perfect.) "Your son knows de Max, he's ruined!" This was their *leitmotiv*, and it was inaccuracy itself. There were no black masses, or pink ones. There were no traps for young men. De Max's private life was more like the family circle of a caravanful of gipsies, and his bedroom was like that of Louis XIV. He received his courtesans, his male favourites and his

. . . spelt terror to any mother

female favourites—the latter, a real harem of delightful women.

From my first visit I have kept a photograph with the dedication: *A vos seize ans en fleur, mes quarante en pleurs,* and the memory of a curious dedication from Mounet-Sully which adorned the bedroom: *A de Max son admirateur admirable.* De Max was as ageless as a cat.

Chieftain, Emir, large Siamese, or black panther, he would curl up in the semi-darkness among the dirty cushions and furs where our sharp eyes recognized the costume of Hippolyte.

Much later I was to know the bric-à-brac at the Marquise Casati's. I prefer her unicorn's horn, stuffed boas, bronze hinds, and mechanical tigers to the nice little audacities of fashion and that good taste which puts yesterday's bad taste on a pedestal and radiates nothing mysterious or significant. A room resembles its occupant. It is the soul's costume, a costume which our soul alters and to which it quickly gives shape. Once it is imposed on the soul a room shapes our behaviour. Tidiness and untidiness do not imitate each other.

Ah, how easily we can imagine your homes, Louisa Casati, you who found no car high enough for your hairstyles; Georgette Leblanc, you who cycled behind Maeterlinck with your Louis XV heels; Jane Catulle-Mendès, you who did your morning shopping in a dress with a train—I love you, I respect women like you, exaggerated, marvellous women, delightful whirlwinds, precursors of the stars!

With de Max untidiness was his style, his acting, the caprices of a warm, generous and oriental nature. In this apartment that was feared and laughed at and formed his being, the examples we received were those of nobility only.

Marie, the elderly maid with Guanhumarah's grey hair, opened the door to the vestibule. The guest went through a series of rooms which owed something to the Fratellinis' dressing-room, a taxidermist's shop and the workroom of Coppélius or Faust. On a pale green upright piano carved with climbing pink roses, were stacks of books—Verlaine, Baudelaire, Verhaeren, and Gide—in bindings as heavy as prayer books. You had to find your way through the fluted columns, Gothic chests and cathedral tapers. Four steps led down to the imitation Pompeii bathroom; to the right a bay window looked on to a sad little Paris garden. A dead hosepipe, a dead lawn and prison walls. An archway separated the bedroom from the writing table. De Max dipped his pen in the mouth of a pottery toad. He wrote in violet ink in tall pointed handwriting, which he dried with gold dust. He kept his money in a little cup and distributed it to anyone who was poorer than he was.

If he went out, he wore a pearl-grey corduroy velvet suit, fastened a pearl-grey tiepin in his black satin cravat, fixed the big grey pearl of his bowler hat over his left ear, put on pearl-grey gloves, dabbed pearly powder over his grey double chin, moistened his yellow-rimmed eyes with saliva, and in his little patent leather boots with their pearl-grey uppers he went out, crossed the courtyard, climbed into his pearl-grey "electric" and there, sitting stiffly upright, revealing to numismatists the coins of his two profiles, he drove in silence towards the Bois de Boulogne. Motionless, he drove round the lake, looking heavenward, with a beauty spot at the corner of his nostril and a bitter mouth, and returned by the same route. In the evening he interpreted plays in eight acts by Ferdinand

Hérold and Paul Vérola: *Bouddha, Ramsès II* and goodness knows what else—all the heroes and all the legends which stimulated his craze for costumes and attitudes.

Since this chapter began with balls I will relate the scandal of the ball given by Robert d'Humières at the Théâtre des Arts, which he directed. De Max, who was the most naïve man in the world, had thought of going with an escort consisting of Rocher, Chiro Vesperto—a model—and me. We were even more naïve than he was. We saw nothing in his plan beyond an excuse for a masquerade.

Imagine, at the door in the Boulevard des Batignolles, the pearl-grey "electric", emitting its passengers before the astonished gaze of Robert d'Humières, de Max wearing an eagle helmet and an Arab veil, Rocher and Vesperto dressed like Arcadian shepherds and myself as Heliogabalus, with auburn curls, an overwhelming tiara, a pearl-embroidered train, rings on my toes and painted nails.

We did not take long to discover our mistake. Robert d'Humières parked us rapidly in an *avant-scène* box where people laughed in our faces. Sarah Bernhardt sent Mlle. Seylor, her companion, to me. "If I were your mother, I would send you to bed." I sniffed back my tears. The black dye from the eye shadow ran over my face and smarted. De Max realized his mistake. He took us away, smoothed out our curls, removed our make-up and took us home.

This was not my only memory of gaiety in which de

L'avant scène
scandaleuse !

. . . "If I were your mother, I would send you to bed"

Max played a part. This large-hearted man, amongst his other errors of taste, committed that of admiring my first poems and of doing them a service.

He organized a reading at the Théâtre Fémina devoted to my poems and paid for it out of his own pocket. The most famous actresses came at his request. Laurent Tailhade combed his grey mane, like that of

Canon Mugnier, fixed his glass eye, his monocle, and read an introductory lecture, a real massacre of the poets of the time. He left me standing alone.

It is none the less true that my beginnings date from that reading and that the efforts I had to make afterwards to have it forgotten were enough to make it unforgettable. But in the end de Max helped me. He read deeper than my silly poems and guessed there was a hidden strength within me, forcing me to conquer myself, and teaching me that grandeur does not easily go hand in hand with delicate nuances.

Hail Isadora Duncan! Hail Mounet-Sully! Hail Sarah Bernhardt! Hail de Max!

They are colossi who should take as their motto the reply made by the Indian chief who was reproached for eating a little too much at table at the White House: "A little too much is just enough for me."

Mon dernier
Souvenir de
Sarah B. dans Athalie

Jean

XI

CATULLE MENDÈS

THE blind man is a tragic figure, the deaf man is comic. You will never make people laugh at a blind husband (in the literal sense), and you will never move them with a deaf one. And yet the deaf are more closed in, more excluded from the world than the blind, and they are sadder. There are blind men who are gay, blind men who amuse themselves; but the deaf man is incurably sad. If you think about it, it is not difficult to recall the past with one's eyes. It is another matter to do so with one's ears. We can easily imagine the setting for a dinner given by Louis XIV; but the sound of the voices, the way of talking, joking and laughing escape us. We can imagine a square in Athens on a festival day and the ladies arriving at the theatre at cock-crow, at six o'clock in the morning, for the première of *Antigone*; but it is impossible to invent the sound of it. The future will probe this emptiness and will discover fragments of fanfares, the chatter of crowds and the declamation of orators. The silence of the past weighs heavily upon us and the music of the Greeks remains a mystery.

If the lines of the drawings which accompany this chapter surprise you, remember that I am not using any caricatures made at the time; I am drawing from memory, trying to keep my writing pen and my drawing pen in the same rhythm. It is not easy. And when I hesitate, when the faces of which I speak remain only a misty likeness, I try to obtain one characteristic which corresponds to my memory. A pen is so ineffective. A sketch is so little. I would like to be able to communicate the sound of dead voices, to break open this unbearable tomb of silence, to take something more than silhouettes from vanished years and by some unimaginable trick make you hear the ha-ha-ha with which Catulle Mendès accompanied the slightest sentence, the muffled organ-voice of Edmond Rostand or the laughter which Proust smeared over his face with his white-gloved hand and his beard.

I knew Catulle Mendès a little before the Théâtre Fémina reading organized by de Max (whom my uncle Raymond Lecomte, who despised "mountebanks" and respected the correct use of the preposition, insisted on calling "the actor Max"). Mendès seemed to him beyond the pale, and he forced my family to share this verdict. I admired Mendès in secret therefore, and did not dare confess an item of news which was to subject my nerves to a severe ordeal; Catulle Mendès, after the Fémina reading, had invited me to luncheon at his home in the boulevard Malesherbes. Keeping this event to myself and waiting for the day almost made me ill. At last the day arrived. And first of all I must try to describe the critic of *Le Journal*, who was feared by the playwrights, was a playwright himself and a poet less read than celebrated.

During that long horrible period when youth seeks

out the last word in refinement and turns against its masters, I happened to laugh at Catulle Mendès and described him without love. I regret it. May his shade find my apologies here. In what better way could I

offer them to him, and how could I pay him homage better than in these souvenir portraits, where I concentrate on visual memories, purposely leaving aside those intimate memories which assail us at the moment of our death?

The palissade of Greta Garbo's eyelashes, the dresses worn by Marlène Dietrich in the Shanghai express and the young men's clothes which these artists wear in private life certainly create a new romanticism. But the sacred monsters of flesh and blood are dying out, and I believe young people nowadays will never again see the likes of such as Catulle Mendès and his wife, or Ernest La Jeunesse or Jean de Bonnefon, his head adorned with thousands of little grey curls looking like frills.

Catulle Mendès in the theatre corridor during the interval! I hardly dare undertake this description, and first of all I must warn you about the danger of confusing emphasis with caricature, and the blackness of an etching with the blackness of the heart. I would like everyone to understand the admiring respect with which I approach a defunct figure who trailed behind him the august ruins of Romanticism and the purple of its gods.

Catulle Mendès was fat and walked lightly. His hips and shoulders undulated. A sort of airship roll propelled him blindly along. The crowd parted in surprise as he passed. He was like a lion and a turbot. His cheeks, eyes and little fish-like, half-moon mouth seemed to be imprisoned in some sort of jelly which kept him at a distance and put some mysterious transparent trembling thickness between him and the rest of the world. He had the same little curls, waves and reddish moustache as a lion, the same proud mane and the same tail, formed by the tails of his black dress suit hanging down below the short putty-coloured coat which was left untidily open. His coat bore the red ribbon of the Legion of Honour and revealed his loose white cravat, his shirt-front stained with coffee, his jacket, his shirt showing between his dress-waistcoat and his trousers which hung in countless folds over tiny pointed boots. In his charming pale plump hands he carried a Chaplinesque walking stick.

And so, with his opera hat upside down, his plaster-cast eyes, his curls hanging down on his high narrow shoulders, his elbows by his side and his cuffs sticking out of his sleeves, Catulle Mendès, the terrible trustee of tomorrow's oracles, followed his corporation, a magnificent and prow-like figure cutting his way through the waves of spectators. He was escorted by Madame Mendès, who was tall, as painted as an idol, and behind the aquarium of her draperies, followed by the frothing drapery of her mandarin sleeves and trains, looked like some marvellous Japanese fish.

De Max had led me towards the couple. Mendès and his wife stopped in the midst of the ebbing tide. De Max introduced me, his illustrious voice penetrating those thick layers which made Mendès inaccessible to timid people, and it was then that Mendès said to me, with his inimitable ha-ha-ha: "Young man, come and share my omelette next Wednesday."

You can imagine that on the following Wednesday I could hardly contain myself and arrived early. I rang. A maid opened the door and asked me what I

... followed his corporation

wanted. More dead than alive, I murmured that I had come to luncheon, and that the master had invited me. The maid let me keep my hat and pushed me into a dark room. Gradually objects came out of the gloom. Simple Chinese furniture, an artistic bronze on the chimney-piece. Between the window and the chimney-piece, a marvellous portrait: Banville by Renoir.

I waited. I waited. At last a door slammed. A discussion . . . and the horrible conviction that Mendès had come home and had forgotten me. It was too late to escape. I remained for a long time alone. All at once a door that I had not been watching opened, and Mendès appeared, most strangely, for he wore a mask, a real carnival mask with a lace border. He excused himself, admitted that he had forgotten me, but said that I should share his luncheon, and explained that he had had a fall the day before on the boulevard Malesherbes. The mask was to keep in place a plaster on his nose.

We went to table. Both in Paris and Saint-Germain (his country house), Mendès adorned his dining-room with an aviary. He was mad about birds, which he collected and called by their names. The birds flew out of their cages, chirped round the sideboards, and pecked crumbs off the tablecloth.

The German chemist Schliemann paid for the luxury of opening up the tombs of Mycene and seeing the Atrides, who were buried standing up, wearing their golden masks. He had barely rejoiced in this costly spectacle when the great corpses vanished into dust. And so, through contact with this man who opened up as the bottles emptied, I saw the great shades of Baudelaire, de Nerval, Rimbaud, Verlaine. Alas, like the Atrides, they consisted only of a golden powder, a mist which left their outlines to the imagination. All the same, I shall never forget that luncheon, that omelette, the ha-ha-ha of the master as he spoke and gesticulated, interpolating dates and anecdotes, yet bringing out of his confused memory a procession of dead kings.

Afterwards I was to lunch with Catulle Mendès every Saturday at Saint-Germain. There were the same birds and the same verbal resurrections, At four o'clock Mendès equipped himself, injected drugs into his eyes and into his thighs through his clothes and yelled as he sprayed himself with Pennès vinegar. Once in motion, he took the train and did not stop again before reaching the *terrasse* of a boulevard café.

His death astounded me. His maid gave me the news by telephone. After dining with his friends the Oppenheims, where he had drunk nothing because of some injury to his pride, he returned in an abnormal state and mistook the tunnel and its lamps for the darkness of the station platform. He fell down and the train crushed him to death.

I went to the Hôtel Meurice to announce the tragedy to the Rostands. I had become very friendly with Maurice, who with François Bernouard and I had founded a magazine called *Schéhérazade*, with a cover that represented a naked Sultana by Iribe, and it was quite simply the first luxury revue reserved entirely for poets. Maurice and I were the young men of the

moment. The era of young men, which was inaugur-
ated by Raymond Radiguet, did not yet exist. We
believed we were Byron and Shelley and that it was

... Maurice and I were the young men of the moment

enough to talk about Oxford and go down the
Champs-Elysées in an open carriage in the April
sunshine.

At Saint-Germain a crowd of people invaded the garden and the vestibule. Mendès rested in a little room reserved for the Larousse. Léon Dierx wept. A sheet concealed the mutilated body and the wax tapers illuminated an admirably beautiful face. The face of a dead man returns to the contours of adolescence. The death mask of Napoleon at Saint-Helena reveals the cheekbones and profile of Bonaparte. In death Mendès looked like Heine, and I remembered a story that I had heard him tell: when he was young he went to see Madame Heine and she collapsed, fainting, for the resemblance was so strong that she believed her crippled husband had found his legs again and walked.

Sarah dans le rôle
de Cyrano
qu'elle joua pour la représentation
en l'honneur de Mendès

XII

THE HÔTEL BIRON

"FROM now on Fantomas" . . . "Fandor retorted" . . . "Agony seized hold of Juve"—the Fantomas style . . . the mocking familiarity of Arsène Lupin . . . the lament in italics of Rouletabille. I should describe the whole period when I lived in the Hôtel Biron in this way.

At that pretentious age when nothing seems worthy of our genius, when no miracle surprises us, when we are convinced that fate owes it to us and has exceptional abodes in store for us, I had the good fortune to live in a huge building with five french windows opening on to a garden of twenty acres in the heart of Paris, in the Boulevard des Invalides. I should say bad fortune, for it is a pity that when we become capable of appreciating it such aggressive good fortune favours us no longer.

One day when I was playing truant from school in the rue de Varenne I went into the enormous courtyard of the house which stands at the corner of the Boulevard des Invalides and asked the concierge if I could look round. I learned that the house was called the Hôtel Biron, that it had last been the Convent of the Sacred Heart, that since the separation of the Church and State it had been in the hands of the custodian of state possessions; Rodin lived in the central part, the

rest was let, and if I would take the trouble to follow
the concierge he would show me the rooms that were
free. If any one of them suited me I had only to make
an offer to M. Ménage, the custodian. That same
evening I was in possession of the room I mentioned,
which had formerly been used by the nuns for music
and dancing classes. I paid as much for it during a
year as one is asked to pay during a month in any
sordid hotel. One door, for which I possessed an
enormous key, opened on to an archway, and the
archway on to a garden. Garden, park, kitchen garden,
Paradise, how can I describe it? Anyone lacking the
jaundiced eye of youth would have fallen over backwards. Did Paris really live, walk, circulate, work and
keep going round such a silence? For although it
existed only through this contrast, the silence none
the less imposed itself more firmly, suppressing the
ear to the benefit of the eye, emanating from the grass
and the trees, stifling the din of a city through that
force of habit which makes silence a privilege of
abandoned gardens. It was, if you like, a spectacle of
silence, a phenomenon arising from the way we nearly
always look at things instead of listening. I mean that
the sound of music distracts us less from looking than
looking distracts us from listening; that looking at
something does not prevent you from hearing music;
and that the visual impression of being a thousand
miles from Paris, in the middle of the country, transported you at the same time into the midst of silence.

On the right of the archway you came in through a
little empty chapel, decorated with lilies and doves,

and then into the room with all its high french windows. A stove, a piano, a divan, a packing case covered
with fabric, a few chairs and oil-lamps soon made the
empty classroom habitable, and from one day to
another I invited my astonished guests into a fairytale
kingdom bordered on the left by the gardens of the
rue Barbet-de-Jouy and on the right by the Boulevard
des Invalides down to the disused church where the
Comte d'Osnowitchnine used to arrange Russian
festivals. I shall never forget Catulle Mendès, who
thought he was visiting some poet in his garret (after
the luncheon in the Boulevard Malesherbes), and came
one evening into surroundings worthy of Capitaine
Fracasse: "Good God, Good God," he repeated,
tapping his legs and my furniture with his cane; he
passed his hand over his face and his yellow curls like
a pianist, recited lines from one of his recent works,
and followed his corporation in its unbuttoned waist-
coat among the clumps of trees and the gates. Chris-
tiane Mancini, my companion of the moment, had
done the shopping in a black velvet dress with a train,
buying bottles of beer and sandwiches in the rue de
Bourgogne. We invited Mendès. The moonlight, as
Madame de Sévigné almost said, arranged its clothes,
statues, penguins and dead nuns. A fabulous mass of
ruins and wild roses formed a perfumed thicket in the
midst of a kind of amphitheatre of sand and weeds.
This was the only place that the brambles and tree
branches had not invaded. The rest formed a small
virgin forest, an inextricable vegetable tangle. The
moss-covered steps, the façade with its green windows,

the sundial-centre of the house (now the Rodin Museum), overlooked this jungle. On the other side my french windows, which were difficult to open because of the thick carpets of scorpion-grass, looked on to real tunnels of green, which led into the unknown.

I am telling you about the accident which made it possible for me to enjoy a domain reminiscent of the Hôtel Pimodan and led us to imitate Baudelaire's receptions because it seems to mark the end of the discoveries that Paris held in store for those who searched through it, like a local flea-market. Later, fate ordained that this place of poetry should be saved by a poet. One morning in fact I heard the custodian talking in the porter's lodge about breaking up the estate and extending the rue de Bourgogne as far as the Hôtel Rohan. I warned the Press. Hallais, Abel Bonnard, Chaumeix and Nolhac came to see me, learning that this treasure existed and at the same time that it was going to disappear. Their articles won the day. Ministers came in their turn and were distressed. In short I saved the gardens of the Hôtel Biron and I am proud of it. I was not so proud in my own home of possessing a fairytale domain, for this bachelor establishment earned me maternal disapproval. A ridiculous incident gave the game away. My mother belonged to the Society of Friends of the Louvre. The Society decided to visit the Hôtel Biron and asked my mother to arrange with her son for the Friends of the Louvre to use his entrance. My mother replied to the president that he must be mistaken, that her sons, etc. . . . Letter followed letter . . . questions were asked . . . and the secret was out. My mother made the best of a bad business and was gracious enough to serve cakes and orangeade on my packing cases on the day of the visit. But alas, I had to renounce the luxury of owning any other home apart from the room that looked on to the courtyard in the Avenue Malakoff.

Long, long afterwards I was to know whose lamp it was that burned every night behind a corner window. It was the lamp of Auguste Rodin's secretary, Rilke. I thought I knew many things and I lived in the crass ignorance of pretentious youth. Success had put me on the wrong track and I did not know that there is a kind of success worse than failure, and a kind of failure which is worth all the success in the world. Neither did I know that the distant friendship of Rainer Maria Rilke would one day console me for having seen his lamp burn without knowing that it was signalling to me to go and singe my wings against its flame.

XIII

A CRITIC AND AN EMPRESS

I OWE many treasures to Lucien Daudet. Apart from his friendship and finding a second family in his family, it was through him that I met the Empress Eugénie, Jules Lemaître and Marcel Proust.

It was during dinner one Sunday in the rue de Bellechasse that I met Jules Lemaître, when Léon Daudet imitated Zola for us and in his lisping way made the remarks Zola would have made concerning contemporary political and literary events. It was not necessary to have known Zola to enjoy this imitation and to react to the shock of it. Léon did not give an imitation, he raised a man from the dead, and it was no longer a joke, but a miracle, something which dominated, frightened and bewitched the whole table. From time to time he dispersed the ghosts with laughter as hearty as a clap on the shoulder. Then the dinner table began to turn and the lisping ghost was tamed, came back and materialized again.

After dinner Reynaldo Hahn went to the piano and sang *L'Ile Heureuse* by Chabrier. Reynaldo sang just as he sang at Madeleine Lemaire's house or in his room in that most mysterious Hôtel des Réservoirs at Versailles, with his cigarette in one corner of his mouth and his exquisite voice in the other, his eyes turned heavenwards, all the little formal garden of his blue

Reynaldo chante "l'île Heureus"

. . . his cigarette in one corner of his mouth and his exquisite voice in the other

cheeks turned towards the darkness, and the rest of him freewheeling down a gentle nocturnal slope behind the piano.

In Touraine, at the Château de La Roche, Lucien became an expert on flowers and gardening. In Paris, in the rue de Bellechasse the flowers were pictures: Madame Alphonse Daudet by Renoir, reminiscent of intoxicating braziers of heliotrope; Lucien by Besnard, a camellia, a gardenia, the flower you wear in your buttonhole at the age when frivolity is permissible; and the famous canvas by Carrière where Daudet resembles a river god bearing off his daughter like Ophelia. Jules Lemaître listened to Léon and Reynaldo. He laughed, and the top of his head turned crimson, his veins swelled and his hands shook like his voice, but he had not yet spoken a single word. It was as we said goodbye, practically in the hallway, that Léon said, "What an extraordinary ambassador Victor Hugo would have been!" Jules Lemaître corrected him: "I don't think he would have been an extraordinary ambassador, but on the contrary he could have been an ambassador extraordinary!" This reply sums up the mind of Lemaître. These fine shades of meaning remain lifeless for foreign or inattentive ears. His mind was set in one direction. Which direction? you may ask. No direction. It was just set, like the pearl in the oyster.

Friendship alone determined the opinions of this great sceptic, and his opinions were extreme because of the strength of his heart. He twisted the fleurs-de-lys of the *Action Française* into a spray and presented them to Léon and his relatives, whom he adored, and

whose cause he supported blindly. His quarrel with
Anatole France dated from the Dreyfus affair. They
were reconciled at a luncheon party given by Marie
Sheikévitch, at which I was present. This reconcilia-
tion took place on the ground of scepticism. They
were both at home there, and apart from a few thrusts
about Joan of Arc, we watched the spectacle of a duet
à la tierce surrounded with Chinese politeness and the
colours of an illuminated missal, between two disciples of Voltaire separated by circumstances which in
no way affected their profound unbelief.

I never went to the Villa Saïd on Sunday morning.
I only saw Anatole France's astonishing long crooked
face in its Gothic surroundings. From skull cap to
beard the face seemed crudely sculpted, following the
curves of some mediæval log or Japanese ivory. On
Sunday mornings I used to go and see Jules Lemaître.
He was not surrounded with courtiers, like Anatole
France. He received me alone. Pauline, his house-
keeper, took me into the library where he worked, an
old glass-panelled studio which occupied almost the
entire floor of the little house in the rue d'Artois. I
went down twelve steps and found myself surrounded
with shelves. Books, books! These were the beams
that shone round Jules Lemaître, and if all Saint
Sebastian's arrows were beams of light, then it is fair
that the beams which surrounded Lemaître were the
beams of library shelves. For his pedagogic soul was
touching, young and fresh. He had to be seen in
Touraine, in his garden sloping steeply down to the
Loire, rejoicing at finding himself in the fresh air again.

Jean Cx

Jules Lemaître

In the rue d'Artois in Paris this wine-grower who had missed his way, this countryman who had been dragged into a city adventure, recalled his vine only by his wine-coloured dressing-gown, his knotty vine-stock silhouette and the tufts of his snow-white hair and head.

I knew the yellow drawing-room where Madame Muhlfeld played the game of chess which consists of making a writer immortal, moving him from square to square and finally placing him under a cocked hat and the dome of the Académie Française. In Jules Lemaître's day it was Madame de Loynes who played the game. Lemaître was her victim and her victory. With this Tourangeau from Tavers she had won the game checkmate. In the place of honour above his chimney-piece a portrait adorned with a bunch of artificial Parma violets testified to her success. Sometimes I stayed to luncheon. If he was in a good mood we lunched cheerfully. I amused Lemaître, I made him feel lighter. He called me Ariel.

A poet believes, and he wants to be believed. This unbeliever could not like poets. He admired Heinrich Heine and those skilful phrases which in the somewhat thick, dry, brown style of Barrès acted like angelica in gingerbread. Of Mallarmé he said, "He is a rose injected with morphine", and of Anna de Noailles, "She's a blackamoor! Her ancestors were gipsies!" At Gougy's he had bought Athenaeus' *Deipnosophistae* in eight volumes, which was too expensive for me. He made me come to his house to read it. "I will leave it to you in my will," he said, "only beware of Anna de Noailles. She's got her eye on it. She's like those insects which carry twigs bigger than themselves. One day you'll see her going secretly out of my house dragging those eight volumes behind her." Had I been an established poet he would have feared me. He would have avoided me or awakened me, as women avoid or awake sleep-walkers. He liked in me the onset of poetry and its harmless manifestations. I think that in the long run poetry would have estranged me from him. Before his death he read a few paragraphs from *Le Potomak*. "I don't understand a word of it," he said, "not one wretched word. *But your prose has a Latin ring to it!*"

He often used to say, "I would like to write an article about you and make contact with journalism again. But I give it up. We live in an age of excesses. We have lost our balance and forgotten the meaning of words. The warmest praise from me would sound cold. People would think I didn't appreciate you."

On the 14th of July, the Comtesse de Noailles, Madame Sheikévitch, Jules Lemaître and I used to dine in the Place de la Bastille at the Quatre Sergents de la Rochelle, with the windows open on to the dancing in the street. It was a rite and a doctrine.

Edmond Rostand joined us at our last meeting. An old misunderstanding had separated the author of *Cyrano de Bergerac* and the critic of *Les Contemporains* ever since the play was performed. This encounter, on the evening of the 14th of July, was a friendly ambush arranged by Anna de Noailles. Jules Lemaître was apparently the only critic who had in no way sounded the fanfare of triumph. He thought that *Cyrano* was the clasp of *La Guirlande de Julie* and had nothing new to say.

Our evening began wonderfully. Rostand tried to charm Lemaître and charmed us. Suddenly Rostand's monocle fell down and broke. The woman at the cash desk pulled a face and asked for one of the pieces which the waiter who was serving us had put in his pocket. Then Rostand took out a second monocle which he gave to her and a third which he fixed in his eye.

Did this number of monocles irritate Lemaître? Was this the last straw? The fact remains that when Rostand burned a hole in the tablecloth with his cigarette and behaved like a small boy, pretending he was frightened and didn't know what to do, Jules Lemaître emerged from his silence and said drily "It's perfectly simple. Autograph the hole."

The fireworks, the shouts of the crowd and the liveliness of Anna de Noailles saved the situation. But that was our last dinner at the Quatre Sergents de la Rochelle.

Lucien introduced me to the Empress Eugénie at Cap Martin, where we were staying in a hotel with our mothers. The Empress owned the Villa Cyrnos, with its steeply-sloping gardens which overlooked the sea, between the property of Madame D, which was infested with croaking frogs, and that of Maria Star. On one side of the wall Maria Star (the pseudonym of Madame S), displayed the chasubles, chains, rings, pendants, croziers and corpulence of a Babylonian bishop; on the other side of the wall lived the most moving and anachronistic woman of the century.

Youth enters and meets age departing. This is an interminable moment, a terrifying minuet which lasts a whole night through. This contact of hands forms a never-ending chain. I had to overcome my shyness and laziness and allow Lucien, a real page-boy in the little court of Cyrnos and Farnborough Hill, to take me to the Empress. It was intensely hot. The crickets hummed like fever and quinine. The sea sparkled and licked itself on the shore.

They say that Tarquinius Superbus lashed at poppies with his whip and cut off their heads—a sign of activity. The Empress detested flowers. She hit them with her stick, pushing them out of her way. We crossed also a dry garden, consisting only of rocks and cactuses. A real Spanish garden with stiff plants, more spiked and bristling than madonnas.

I was beginning to lose countenance, to fear the apparition which would not be long delayed (the Empress was out walking and we were going to meet her), and to imagine Winterhalter's *Decameron*—the Empress, seated in the midst of her maids of honour, a thousand times less reassuring than the grenadiers of the guard—when the meeting took place, rapid and unexpected, as dark and small as an accident. And, as with an accident I had all the leisure, watching the obstacle slowly approach, to control my nerves, feel no emotion and not lose my head.

The Empress came out of a winding alley. Mme. de

Mora and the Comte Clary, who were in attendance, appeared afterwards. Wearing a sort of cassock and a priest-like hat she climbed up, leaning on a stick like some goat fairy. What struck me first was the small amount of space she occupied, reduced in size like those heads that were shrunk by the savages who killed her son; she was a blot of ink in bright sunshine. And I realized that all that remained of this Mont-golfier balloon was the charred petrol tank, the black heart of the poppy. The things that were missing with which one normally associated her were the crinoline, the boating-jacket, the spencer, the dangling ribbons, the huge swaying straw hat, the crown of wild flowers and the tiny broken umbrella from Chantilly.

The face was the same. It had kept its delicate oval shape. It looked as though an unhappy young woman had buried her face in her hands too often and that in the end the shape of her fingers had left their mark upon it. The eyes had kept their heavenly blue but the gaze had been diluted. An expanse of blue water inspected you. This blue, and the black eye-shadow which underlined it, recalled the tattooed eyes of young sailors who are released from prison when they are old. In these old men you find to your surprise the indelible signs of angry beauty.

The Empress stopped: the blue water looked me up and down. Lucien introduced me. "I can no longer decorate poets," she said; "here you are, I can give you this"—and with a rapid movement she tore off a white bunch of daphne, offered it to me, watched me put it in my button-hole and went on with her walk.

"Come." I walked beside her. She questioned me about dancing—Isadora Duncan and the Ballet Russe. She told me about a firework display the night before at Cap d'Ail. She stopped and sometimes she burst out laughing. That voice, and that laughter which broke in two and threw her backwards—where had I heard them before? It is a memory of the bull-ring—the laughter and chatter of the young Eugénie de Montijo which were to frighten and fascinate the shy Napoleon III, the laughter and chatter of all young Spanish women, stamping with their little goat-like feet and fluttering their fans as they applaud the matador making a kill.

"Preceded by her suite." This little joke would hardly have had any meaning at Cyrnos. The Empress exhausted her attendants, trotted along, was surprised that people complained of tiredness and suggested accompanying me part of the way back.

When I took my leave and she invited me to return soon, I saw a flash of youth illuminate her whole face and her whole frail mourning-clad figure, like the lightning-flash of the salamander which gives life to ruins.

I saw the Empress again at the Hôtel Continental, where stupid people reproached her for staying opposite the Tuileries. What could remain from the past to affect a woman who had died several times, but habit? The habit of living in a certain district, which is stronger than any other.

The Continental preserves the style. The electricity hides beneath the gas-globes of the lamp-stands.

Lucien Daudet led me through the halls with their Boulle furniture and velvet sofas. A brown door with gold markings opened. At the end of a huge drawing-room the Empress was seated, warming herself. The old Comtesse de Pourtalès and the Duc de Montmorency stood by her side; the Duc was wrinkled and cadaverous, covered with moss and lichen, his opera-hat under his arm, prodigious in bearing and elegance.

The Empress had heard that women were wearing coloured wigs. She questioned me. I replied that this was so, but that I rarely visited the places where one saw them. The Comtesse de Pourtalès was horrified: "Coloured wigs! They must be mad." Then the Empress turned round all at once. "My dear," she cried, "we have done other things in our time!" And as the old lady began to contradict her sovereign as far as she might, the Empress, implacable, hoarse and childish, began to rehearse the list of their follies. The crinoline, inspired by Goya's Infantas, the linen pantalettes which showed beneath dresses, tasselled boots, she forgot nothing. And finally, "You, my dear, you had a carriage with glass panels and roses painted on them." The Comtesse choked: "With roses painted on them!" The Empress was much amused. She was precise. She insisted. The Duc was entirely of her opinion, he unearthed old scandals, old jokes, and old eccentricities. I neither breathed nor moved, trembling lest by some clumsy gesture I should interrupt this astonishing scene, lest I should close the Empress's drawer sharply, make the cock crow and send the ghosts away.

XIV

ANNA DE NOAILLES

LUCIEN DAUDET, Mauriac and I formed a little group and we were rarely separated. We liked most of all the poetry readings given by fashionable ladies. We never missed one of them. On Tuesdays all these bacchantes met at the Duchesse de Rohan's house, she whose strange genius forced even such as Max Jacob, Claudel and Proust to learn some of her lines by heart.

Dorchain had just published an article in *Les Annales* in which he wrote about these ladies. Apart from the Comtesse de Noailles, he called them all amateurs. This article infuriated them. In the midst of an extravagantly dressed group the Baronne de B, rolling her r's, cried "Amateurs, Amateurs! *We who don't count the feet on our fingers any more!*"

I was to know Madame Simone before knowing the Comtesse de Noailles, and this was logical. Nobody could better prepare me for this encounter with the poet than the actress who served her and recited her poems. What is more, Simone shared with the Comtesse the privilege of words; with her warm clear voice, hastening her delivery or lingering on certain consonants, as precise as a sewing machine and as serious as a viola, the great Bernstein actress excelled in recounting, describing and visualizing what she had seen. Like all those who know how to use their eyes and whose listeners believe they are embroidering, she possessed a genius for exactitude, so dear to the truly imaginative. You will hear it said that Mme. de Noailles never listened to anyone. This is not true. Both she and Simone were wonderful listeners. They understood divinely the regal politeness of listening. Since they were always ready to begin their cantilena and firework display again, why prepare themselves while their partner was talking? They knew how to be all ears. The Comtesse screwed up her face as though she were deaf, cupped her hand and pushed up her black hair; Simone punctuated her silences with "No! Impossible! It's not true", which broke into one's story, encouraged one to continue and afforded proof of sustained attention.

And the laughter! That crazy laughter! How we laughed together! I remember staying at Trie-Château, the country estate of the Casimir-Perier's, when this mad laughter went on and began again, split our sides and gave us cramp and forced us to sit down on the stairs before we could return to our rooms. Alain-Fournier was publishing *Le Grand Meaulnes*. Simone was directing his short-sighted dreams.

"The laughter we shall laugh no more." It is stifling hot. The grass buzzes. The stream flows by. Lying flat beside the cool water, whom do I see? Claude Casimir-Périer: dead. Alain-Fournier: dead. Péguy: dead. They laugh, we laugh. Simone talks and listens. An abject cyclone threatens us.

. . . Sometimes, after the mad laughter, the windows

grew dim; the twilight brought calm. Then Péguy recited stanza after stanza by Victor Hugo. He stopped and Simone began. With her eyes lowered, and her hands clasped round her knees she would recite one of those immense poems that young graduates know by heart: *Tu seras mort ainsi que David, qu' Alexandre* . . .

Who would have suspected that the uneasiness of *Meaulnes*, the acrobat-somnambulist Franz de Galais and the Eugène drawings in *Le Potomak* which were sketched between J.-E. Blanche's home at Offranville and Trie, announced the worst and warned us to be on our guard?

Simone introduced me to Anna de Noailles in a car. She was coming away from some lecture or other. At first sight I admit that she astounded me. The Comtesse was used to shining, playing a part and performing exercises that had become famous, and thanks to the credit which I enjoyed through Simone, she treated me, without the slightest preliminary, to a display which was a matter of course to her intimate friends but which was enough to make any new spectator feel like a provincial.

I must have looked like a frock-coated Fratellini beneath a shower of hats in the midst of one of those scenes of carnage which leave the circus ring strewn with old guitars, broken furniture, soap lather, saucepans and broken china.

Gradually I became used to it. The beauty of this little person and the graceful sound of her voice, combined with an extraordinarily amusing power of description, triumphed over everything else, and I understood once and for all that the way she sniffed and leant back, crossed her legs, stopped, opened her

. . . The Comtesse is talking

hands and flung them away from herself as though from a sling, the gestures which strewed the floor with veils, scarves, collars, Arabian beads, muffs, handkerchiefs, miniature umbrellas, belts and safety pins, constituted her décor, her driving-power and in some way the accessories to her act.

I admit that as soon as I felt developing between us one of those friendships that last beyond the grave, I surrounded myself with all imaginable precautions. At table she wanted all the guests to listen to her and remain silent. I have elsewhere quoted that remark of Baudelaire's: "Hugo launches himself into one of those monologues that he calls conversation." The Comtesse, even before going to table, took hold of a conversation of this type and would not let it go. If she drank she would hold her glass in her right hand and made a sign with her left that she must not be interrupted. And the guests obeyed. Hostesses "offered" her and repeated the *leitmotiv* "Anna is wonderful! Wonderful!" The Comtesse went on. Going from her maid to George Sand, from her valet to Shakespeare, she juggled, walked up and down the tight-rope, changed from one trapeze to another and performed conjuring tricks. Let us admit, and it is now that my precautions begin, she sometimes cheated, lifting cardboard weights and falling off the wire. Some did not notice, some laughed in their sleeves, and others suffered. I was among the latter. I pitied her, I saw her getting into difficulties, becoming muddled and taking short cuts. Anything rather than return to silence! A sort of madness of the tongue, some verbal vertigo prevented her from realizing her folly. After several experiences (sometimes she succeeded and did not slip), I decided that

I would never meet her in public and would only see her in private.

And yet . . . and yet . . . Since I am letting myself go

. . . A sort of madness of the tongue

and proving my brotherly love by giving up the detestable habit of praise which, when it is taken too far, can cause a great deal of harm, I remember one

evening that was profoundly successful. It was at the
Princesse de Polignac's house. I liked the Princesse.
I liked her way of coyly grinding out irrevocable
judgments, accompanying them with a veiled smile and
wagging her head like a malicious young elephant,
I liked her magnificent profile, like a rock worn away
by the sea. And it was certainly because the evening
finished at her house that we had the good fortune
to see Anna de Noailles in full possession of her
faculties.

The evening was coming to an end. On the light-
coloured Savonnerie carpet, the music-stands and the
listeners' chairs stood about untidily. All at once,
among this musical wreckage, I saw the Comtesse de
Noailles sitting surrounded by a group of ladies. She
was devoting herself to extraordinary exercises. The
nightingale practises before the singing season. He
croaks, lows and squeaks and those who are not aware
of his methods are amazed, as they stand at the foot of
the night-dark tree. The Comtesse began in the same
way. I watched her from a distance. She sniffed,
sneezed, burst out laughing, heaved heart-rending
sighs and dropped Turkish necklaces and scarves.
Then she took a deep breath, and, curling and un-
curling her lips at full speed, she began. What did she
say? I no longer know. I know that she talked and
talked and talked and the big room filled with a crowd
of people and the young ones sat on the floor and the
older ones sat in armchairs anywhere. I know that the
Princesse de Polignac and the Princesse de Caraman-
Chimay (her friend and her sister), standing on her left

and her right, seemed to be seconds in some dreamland boxing-ring. I know that the servants in their black suits and the footmen in knee-breeches and powdered wigs put their ears to the half-open doors. I know that through the open windows of June, like the waltz in a film by Lubitsch or in that film where Liszt played the piano, the words of the Comtesse bewitched the trees, the plants and the stars—that these words penetrated into the neighbouring buildings, interrupted quarrels, enriched sleep, and that everything and everyone, from the star to the tree, from the tree to the chauffeurs of the waiting limousines, murmured "The Comtesse is talking . . . the Comtesse is talking . . . the Comtesse is talking. . . ."

Poor dear proud creature! She would have suffered too much from our rapid, disrespectful and inattentive era. Could even Wilde have devised an apologia for it? I doubt it. "Once upon a time . . ." Everyone turns away. Conversations begin again. Gossip starts offbeat. Elbows jostle against one another. Legs touch. Wilde stops short, alone and haggard, with a crimson carnation in his hand.

Further. I have been told that the Comtesse was the victim, during her last months, of just such a lack of appreciation. At the house of F.M., at the head of a tea-table surrounded by elegant young women, she had tried to take the reins. A complete waste. The silly young creatures interrupted her right in the middle of a sentence, laughed at her, treating her (no more, no less) like a gambler at Monte Carlo.

The Comtesse grew smaller, pale and hollow-cheeked, like those Chinese nightingales which fall down flat at the bottom of their cages with their wings outstretched and die of an apoplectic fit.

Once more I was to see the Comtesse in public and in top form. She had to meet Francis Jammes at Madame Alphonse Daudet's home in the rue de Bellechasse. Jammes was coming to spend a week in Paris. He wore a snuff-coloured suit, a red tie and beige gaiters. With his beard floating in the wind, his spectacles set for battle, and his cheeks bulging, this superb vermeil triton navigated from group to group with an escort of young spiritualists, sounding an astonishing nasal trumpet. The Comtesse entered. Leaning backwards, wearing a poppy-trimmed straw hat, she stretched out her hands and inspected Jammes. He took hold of her little hands, bent down over the straw hat and repeated "The great lady! Here is the great lady!"

Some of Jammes' poems were recited. He shuddered like a horse shooing flies away, waggled his thigh like an examiner and, with one leg crossed over the other, shook his pale-gloved foot like a hand. The Comtesse whispered to me: "Just look! The vet who has cured a human being!" And a few days later (I had asked her for a description of Jammes' visit), "We talked about the weather. It was no change from our books."

She fired these cracks like a machine-gun. Nobody could aim better. Provided the spectators did not upset her and make her disastrously dizzy, she scored a bull's eye each time. Egg or eagle, she never missed.

And after shooting down the eagle you could expect her to say, like the Austrian archduke, "What, has it only one head?" For this intuitive woman imagined that she had the culture of a Goethe. The astonishing electricity which escaped from her, the lightning which played about her, the waves which emanated from her, she persisted in taking all this for intelligence. As for the naïveté of genius, she would have none of it. Mme. de Montebello's remark, "Anna looks at Versailles with the eyes of Zamore", disgusted her. This disgust formed the theme of long intimate sessions "behind the curtains"; this was the expression which described our custom of avoiding each other outside and of meeting only at her house, 40 rue Scheffer.

Ginet, the old servant, stank of the cellar. He propelled me in zigzags towards a padded door, which opened into a little room of silence, the end of a corridor which intercepted sounds; the walls were lined with books and cork, and the carpets rested on cottonwool. This dark silence preceded a second padded door. The bedroom door. I went in. Anna de Noailles received her guests reclining on a wide Louis XV bed. The room was that of a young girl in about 1900. The only contrast was an enlarged photograph of Minerva, her forehead resting against her lance. Leaning stiffly to one side, helmet on head, like a figure seven, she stood in meditation. But this pensive Minerva was not Anna's patron, who was more likely to be the turbulent Pallas of the *Aeneid,* the grasshopper from the Acropolis, the sacred hill from

where the Musurus tribe brought her down. Indeed
it was not Anna, this little leaning-column Minerva.
It was not she whom Maurras would embrace in the
Parthenon. Maurras classes the young countess-poet
with the *"magots"*, those primitive ladies in the

. . . received guests reclining on a wide Louis XV bed

Acropolis museum who recline on their tombs, their
smiling faces consumed by their eyes, beside their
bearded husbands. What a contrast—like that between
the bedroom and Minerva—between these yellow
ribbons, laces, cretonnes, the furniture with twisted
legs, these trinkets of all types and the lady of the
house! Her raven-wing hair, a catogan and a long curl
(she called it her Colonne Vendôme) descending in

spirals over her shoulders, and her large eyeballs looking as though they were painted on a band covering her eyes so that she had to raise her head to look out from underneath. These artificial eyes, these huge eyes, streamed out right and left from her horizontal face. A strong nose, like a beak, and deep-cut nostrils powerful enough to breathe in all the scents in the world. The graceful mouth, with lips curling like rose petals, revealed the jaws of a carnivore. This framework and animal-like bone structure illustrated the remark of Lemaître. What a delightful insect! The microscope reveals an arsenal of saws, pincers and antennæ.

What in her passing put me in mind of the sublime death of the scorpion who thrusts a dagger into itself, surrounded by flames?

Born for the grass and for "a rose tree to spring from her bones", born to be dead, she could not bear the glowing bonfire of the old world and its threatening flames. She was weary.

She liked crimson, the sign of power. This woman who was in love with Jaurès suspended the sabre of Mangin at the foot of her bed.

It was fame that she worshipped. Fame, her *idée fixe!* "You only admire second-raters," she said to me. In vain did I demonstrate to her that the privilege of France was precisely the possession of secret glories, famous men of whom the mass know nothing. Rimbaud is hardly known. Verlaine only just. Hugo's fame lies in the number of his squares, streets and avenues. In the eyes of the Comtesse, fame, Rome and

the number of His temples were one of the proofs of
the existence of God. "Anna," I said to her, "you want
to be a statue during your lifetime, a statue with legs
to run about everywhere." When she insulted me I
answered back, but our quarrels ended by my running
away. I would leave the table. The Princesse de
Polignac used to remember how she once went to
look for me and found me playing draughts with
Anne-Jules, the Comtesse's son. One evening—
the quarrel arose out of my letter to Jacques Maritain
—the Comtesse, in a long nightgown, pursued me,
brandishing a chair, out on to the landing. She leant
over, grasping the banisters and cried, "In any case,
it's straightforward. If God exists, I would be the first
person to be told."

Affectionate quarrels, pretexts for interminable
discussions. Most frequently I attacked her for her
conventional conception of greatness.

She reproached me for losing dash. Love is not
dashing, I replied. Love destroys dash. We say "I love
you"; but the moment I select certain people or things,
when I am ready to die for them, I lose the power of
speech and all its range. A great musician does not
serve music; it serves him. That is why it is preferable
to listen to him playing second-rate music. Then he
can shine. You shine for lack of love, I told her. Your
love is countless and it is nothing. At least you have
not committed the crime of manufacturing love, like
Barrès. Then the quarrel would start again with
redoubled strength. And I would leave. I would go
down the rue Cortambert. Opposite the Hôtel Polignac

in the Avenue Henri-Martin, the asphalt, swollen by the sunshine, absorbed air and formed into a pair of bellows, uttering bird-like cries at night as you walked over it. This detail, and these cries from the pavement, were the last things that woke me and distracted me from my dreams. I went on with the quarrel alone. My heart raged, loved and adored—and since time is invented by men, I would find myself instantaneously, without having walked, in the rue d'Anjou in front of my door.

At the window of the cretonne-hung room a box full of hyacinths formed an obstacle that the Comtesse did not surmount. As she always lay stretched out I believe (unless she breathed in the heliotrope scents of Amphion) that she imagined gardens, flowers, and bumble-bees fringed with hair like the eyes of a Persian princess, through this box of hyacinths, those perfumed sentinels that watched, standing stiffly upright, over her light, rare sleep. She slept badly, stuffed herself with sleeping tablets, felt ill and rarely spoke of her sufferings. People believed that she was a malingerer. Marcel Proust was treated as one. To say "I am dead" instead of "I am tired" is imagination. Poets are imaginary invalids. And they die. How surprising! How inconvenient! People think we are made of steel.

Anna saw a thousand doctors. Apart from Mme. Lobre, whom she loved and believed, the doctors were excuses for vocal exercises. She did not want her doctors to look after her. She wanted to look after her doctors.

She is dead. Life is dead. She of whom Barrès said, "She is the most sensitive spot in the universe". He spoke too of "her little body that looked like a Spanish Christ". She wanted to be embalmed. I did not dare to see her in that state. I can imagine that, embalmed, she must be like Thaïs in the Musée Guimet. Among a rustling and crackling of old cigars, dry roses and dry bandages, Thaïs floats on her back on the river of the dead. One morning, at the Musée Guimet, I saw a Carmelite priest kneeling by the glass case. He carried the heart and cross of Père de Foucauld. It was Père Charles. He was praying. I had forgotten that the mummy was that of Saint Thaïs.

When I die I shall go to see Anna de Noailles. I shall cross the hallway of clouds. I shall open the door and I shall hear the voice reserved for quarrels: "My dear, you see, there is nothing afterwards, nothing. You remember, I told you so"—and to my eternal delight, everything will start all over again. The Comtesse is talking.

XV

DANCING ON THE VOLCANO

ONE should not be angry with those who record their memories with a hasty pen and make mistakes. They write not what was but what is, what remains of what they have lived; and they work behind mists which obscure the outlines. To be pedantic about an error is to be angry about a fairground photograph because it shows you as a boxer, motorist or toreador. "That's not him! That's not her!" What is more, the instinctive choice of décor tells something about the model.

I will add that I live too far away to correct my proofs. Journalism hastens onwards, its pilgrim staff adorned with printer's errors. You will understand that it is not my fault if commas get out of place and change the meaning of a phrase, or if a singular becomes a plural. In the sunshine of Villefranche I watch for these strokes of bad luck and they hurt me. (Madame de Sévigné wrote: "I rely on the reader's good grace. His eye will make the corrections for me.")

History consists of inexactness. It is like that skull by Holbein. From near at hand and from in front marks and lines are elongated. You have to stand at a distance, at the correct angle, for the marks to come together and co-ordinate themselves, allowing the skull to be seen. The details do not matter much. Only masses and volumes and the general lines count, in men or deeds.

One must also be careful about the phenomenon of abstract perspective which makes events, people and places grow bigger as they recede from us. If they gain in lyricism they lose in the relief which can move us. The painters' Golgotha lifts up the cross and makes Christ recede. Catherine Emmerich brings him close, restores the cross and the bare mountain to reasonable proportions, reminding us what a nail that goes through flesh is like.

It is therefore through a judicious blending of great and small that the memoir-writer obtains his likeness. Why go over the account book again and again? We can hardly imagine the queen of the Amazons writing "Alexander's sweat did not smell of violets". The historian could reply "Perhaps your husband arranged not to sweat in your presence" or "You didn't live together very long", for example.

My newspaper work involved serious obstacles. I had to pass from one colour to another, and never let myself be tempted by the pleasant way things follow on from each other, by the rainbow of colours as they merge on the necks of pigeons and asparagus stalks. I have had to avoid the temptation to be moved, to linger, to complain, to boast, to open my heart. I have had to reflect like mirrors which do not reflect, take mirrors out of my pocket and put them back quickly, carry away blindly the impression made by a boxer on the boxing-ring towel, the reflection of a smile in the corner or a mirror, and outline with a pencil the shadow of a profile on the wall.

And then what? Exactness? Inexactness? Solomon's bees, how can you find your way about on our crown of everlasting flowers?

A gentleman whose writing paper is adorned with engraved commonplaces: Legion of Honour—decorations—telephone—telegraph—reproaches me for using commonplaces which are found everywhere. I should blush for shame if journalism did not show me the example, and if the light style it demands did not include the use of commonplaces, some inexcusable, others magnificent, solid on their plinths, made of pure marble, real *chefs-d'œuvres* of the centuries. Were they born? Did they spring, fatherless, from the excavated soil?

Should a farmer rediscover the arms of the Venus de Milo, to whom would they belong? To the farmer or the Venus de Milo? They belong to myth. They encircle the neck of poetry. They are white serpents with a life of their own.

What a delight it is to use "Furthermore—Let me add—I say—besides—in short", all those phrases which fit into place of their own accord like the easy piece of the puzzle!

Forgive me, reader. Understand me. Help me. Play with me. Do not remain standing before my table. It is fitting that we should write and read this sharply-etched prose together.

I owe these souvenir portraits to Gide, if in fact they deserve to live. Gide reproached me (*à propos* a note to *Le Coq et l'Arlequin* on early jazz) for never letting myself go, never relaxing. Writing with one's own blood and shouting one's love by chalking on the walls make pauses necessary. I have argued too much against the sublime not to be suspicious of it.

Just as I owe these articles to Gide, I owe *Les Enfants Terribles* to Jacques Chardonne. He scolded me: "You have masterpiece cramp. White paper paralyses you. Begin with anything. Write: 'One winter evening . . .' and go on." (A phrase like the one which begins my film: *Tandis que tonnaient au loin les canons de Fontenoy, dans une modeste chambre, un jeune homme* . . . a phrase in which the disciples of Freud saw hidden meanings but which expresses nothing beyond the courageous setting in motion of a work.) I wrote: "*La cité Monthiers se trouve prise entre la rue d'Amsterdam . . .*" and the book which must have been waiting within me slid into place behind, in one piece.

And now I am choking with everything I have not said. I do not speak of the essential things which must remain unsaid but of silhouettes which deserve to take their places at the photographer's door.

Have I told you about No. 8 and No. 10 in the rue d'Anjou? No. 8 where La Fayette died and where Edmond Sée occupied Sacha Guitry's apartment. Sacha was our next-door neighbour. I went downstairs four at a time. I dashed past the door on the first floor

—the door of Mme. de Guermantes where I shall soon
describe Proust standing guard—I passed under one
archway after another and I climbed Sacha's spiral
staircase. At the top a life-size caricature by me showed
visitors where the bell was. I gave the agreed number

madeleine Carlier

of knocks and I entered with delight the home of the
man who made the dull town lighter and chased gloom
away, carrying the treasure of French good humour
balanced on his nose, in the midst of the bad humour
of a Paris which is always grumbling. Sacha was
painting the L.S.K. poster. This clown and his
draughtsboard were to gain a celebrity that we hardly
anticipated. We lived, we were happy, gay, and
unconcerned with calculation.

Sacha's only calculation consisted of standing up at his desk and writing in one night scintillating plays, where he appeared only in the second act wearing a dressing-gown. Like this Charlotte Lysès left first and we drank our coffee without hurrying.

Iribe, dubbed Brother Iribus! Madeleine Carlier! Can Iribe remember our visit to the former *Témoin* in the Place de la Bourse? I dare not describe my suit, my tie or my gaiters. I carried under my arm one of Madeleine's white Pomeranians. At Mme. Lanvin's she improvised suits out of Indian shawls and caps with ostrich feathers copied from Directoire fashion plates. A strange couple, I can assure you! Shall I admit that I have kept the soul I had at that time and that I am sometimes astonished at losing contact with other souls which learnt how to grow and become beautiful? As for Sacha and Iribe, we cannot meet each other without a flood of memories rising to our lips and our hearts.

I have mentioned eccentric clothes. At Tiarko Richepin's wedding I was best man along with Maurice Rostand and Mlles. Luro, the bride's sister and cousin. I wore a morning coat, a top hat and a purple carnation (*sic*). The tradesmen laughed as I went by and my mother, at the window in the Avenue Malakoff, wept on seeing how ridiculous I looked. Sacha (whom I did not yet know) took part in the procession on the arm of Cora Laparcerie; he was in the uniform of a new recruit for he was doing part of his military service. Sacha and Tiarko were composing an operetta *Tell Père, Tell Fils*, a tune from which, *Je suis concierge du palais*, was played slowly on the organ as a wedding march. In the silence the words came into our heads and the procession shook with suppressed laughter.

Why, one autumn evening, several years later, did I have the absurd idea of putting on a false Father Christmas beard and roaming among the trees in the Hôtel Biron grounds in the twilight, pretending to be Rodin, whom Tiarko wanted to meet? My imitation made him think at first that Rodin had become senile, and when I shouted to him "Tiarko! Tiarko! It's I, Jean!", he thought that Rodin was going mad and fled from my garden as fast as he could run.

At Sacha's house, near Honfleur, which was famous through *La Pélerine Ecossaise*, a similar prank almost misfired. Sacha and I gave a vague imitation of our dear Dr. Mardrus and his wife. We arrived unexpectedly. Now Ajalbert feared and avoided the Mardrus family. "Too late," cried Charlotte Lysès, "they're coming in", and the misunderstanding began. The worse he played his part, and the more I laughed beneath my veils, the more poor Ajalbert, blind with embarrassment, believed in us, and thought he was being treated impudently.

I would like to write twice as much, gossip and tell stories. What, for example, is this dress Lysès wears in *Nono*? These broad black and white stripes, this green turban, this Empire waist? A vital signature has made its mark on the light heart of the town. The signature of Paul Poiret.

Already the stiffness of Polaire and the Lianes has

relaxed. The corsets are unlaced. The gilt of the theatre boxes no longer frames cocottes in armour and dog collars. All these implacable lines melt away, the

. . . the transitional period

boxes sink, giving way to the typical box of the transitional period. It looks like a dessert of meringues and ice-cream: Edwards, the artist, stands up; ecto-plasm issues from his soft shirt and forms into a shape-less mass, like a female Eugène with splendid eyes, poodle curls and a carp-like mouth: it is Lanthelme.

The duchesses are ready for Paul Poiret to dress

Poiret approche en silence

. . . The duchesses are ready

them, undress them and put them in costume. Mothers
are revolted by Iribe's album. There is no question yet
of pushing out the stomach, walking like a crab and
a praying mantis, putting one hand on the hip and
making the jaw-line cruel and disdainful. It is a
question of being an almeh, a bag of silk and fur, a
lamp shade, a cushion from the harem of a fashionable
sultan. A pale sultan, an emir with a chestnut beard and
protruding eyes, an actor like Nero, changing women
into odalisques and capable himself of incarnating
innumerable types with the rags that he picks up round
about him. Derain must remember how on armistice
night Poiret disguised himself, metamorphosed himself, and invented, mimed and conjured up so much
and so well that at dawn we thought it was 11 o'clock
at night, like those travellers in the German ballad
who were victims of the nightingale.

And there we are. I would prefer to leave you
quickly. I detest stations, and the starting train which
unwinds the skein of the heart.

Like the cedar in Jussieu's hat, Pepito Soto and
Manolo Martinez bring the tango in the box of a
gramophone. From the villa Montmorency (between
Bergson and Gide) the tango was going to invade
Europe. Couples knotted together, their shoulders
motionless, executed the slow Argentinian promenade.
Fat gentlemen glided along with small steps, up and
down, facing their partner. From time to time they
stopped, turned round, raised one foot and inspected
the sole of their shoe as though they had stepped in
something nasty.

... as though they had stepped in something nasty

And here is the fox-trot and the *Très moutarde* and those elegant women with aggressive elbows who bound up and down to *Sambre-et-Meuse*.

The earth shudders. More sensitive than the frivolous vermin who inhabit it, it senses, like a cow, the storm that is gathering in the east. Old and young rub against each other and jump. The earth shakes and disturbs them.

From a distance we are always surprised that art superimposes itself on catastrophes which seem to annihilate it. On the contrary. The stupid crowd turn